SEPHARDIC BALABUSTA SHARES TASTEFUL TREASURES

RECIPES FROM JEWISH COMMUNITIES OF THE MEDITERRANEAN

YAFFA TURGEMAN

CONTENTS

SOUPS & SALADS

VEGETABLES & SIDE DISHES

MAIN DISHES

DESSERTS

COOKIES & CANDY

THIS & THAT

USEFUL NOTES

Saba Avraham and Savta Rachma Turgeman

This cookbook is dedicated to my beloved Father Avraham Turgeman, whom I don't remember as he passed away at a young age, and to my beloved Mom who taught me that family is everything and food is a bridge.

Sabah Avraham and Savtah Zoharah Honouna

This cookbook is also dedicated to my in-laws for always welcoming us with a table filled with tasty salads and savory entrees that were devoured. In this picture Savtah Zoharah is making the Mofletta, to celebrate the Mimouna, the traditional ending of Passover in the Moroccan Jewish community.

Yaffa Turgeman Hanouna—Sephardic Balabusta, Chef, Author, Cooking channel, Restaurateur, Culinary Instructor, Food blogger

When asked how I learned to cook my answer was always, well, I am the youngest of 10 siblings, there was no room for me in house, so, I was always in my mom's kitchen.

WELCOME FRIENDS!

Join me on this food journey to the Jewish communities of the Mediterranean region. I invite you to try a lemon dip from my own previous restaurant, get a refreshing salad from the Greek islands, fish balls from Tunisia, Italian Pasta classico and Moroccan pastia. I included many of my restaurant's favorites and desserts from my private collection which is also featured on my YouTube channel.

Enjoy and share with family and friends, after all food is a bridge, so let's build that bridge together.

Love, Yaffa, the Sephardic Balabusta

Recipe Symbols
🏅—Award Winning
❤️—Heart Healthy
🌶️—Hot & Spicy
🌺—In Memory
⏰—Quick & Easy
🫕—Slow Cooker

WELCOME FRIENDS!

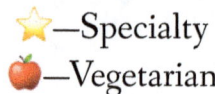—Specialty
🍎—Vegetarian

APPETIZERS
& BEVERAGES

HELPFUL HINTS

- Add flavor to tea by dissolving old-fashioned lemon drops or hard mint candies to it. They melt quickly and keep the tea brisk.
- Make your own spiced tea or cider. Place orange peels, whole cloves, and cinnamon sticks in a 6-inch square piece of cheesecloth. Gather the corners and tie with a string. Steep in hot cider or tea for 10 minutes; steep longer if you want a stronger flavor.
- Always chill juices or sodas before adding them to beverage recipes.
- Calorie-free club soda adds sparkle to iced fruit juices and reduces calories per portion.
- To cool your punch, float an ice ring made from the punch rather than using ice cubes. It appears more decorative, prevents diluting, and does not melt as quickly.
- Place fresh or dried mint in the bottom of a cup of hot chocolate for a cool and refreshing taste.
- When making fresh lemonade or orange juice, one lemon

yields about 1/4 cup juice, while one orange yields about 1/3 cup juice.

- Never boil coffee; it brings out acids and causes a bitter taste. Store ground coffee in the refrigerator or freezer to keep it fresh.
- Always use cold water for electric drip coffee makers. Use 1-2 tablespoons ground coffee for each cup of water.
- How many appetizers should you prepare? Allow 4-6 appetizers per guest if a meal quickly follows. If a late meal is planned, allow 6-8 appetizers per guest. If no meal follows, allow 8-10 pieces per guest.
- If serving appetizers buffet-style or seating is limited, consider no-mess finger foods that don't require utensils to eat.
- Think "outside the bowl." Choose brightly colored bowls to set off dips or get creative with hollowed-out loaves of bread, bell peppers, heads of cabbage, or winter squash.
- Cheeses should be served at room temperature— approximately 70°.
- To keep appetizers hot, make sure you have enough oven space and warming plates to maintain their temperature.
- To keep appetizers cold, set bowls on top of ice or rotate bowls of dips from the fridge every hour or as needed.

AWARD WINNING HUMMUS 🏅 —AWARD WINNING

1/2 teaspoon ground cumin

2 2/3 cups chickpeas (Garbanzo beans)

1/2 teaspoon baking soda

1 small garlic clove, peeled

1/2-3/4 teaspoon salt

1/2 cup freshly squeezed lemon juice

1/2 cup raw tahini (not roasted seeds)

1/2 cup ice water

For decoration—
1 tablespoon harissa, schug, lightly toasted pine nuts
1-2 tablespoons cold press olive oil
2 tablespoons fresh chopped parsley
2 tablespoons cooked chickpeas.

For the authentic recipe use only dry chickpeas, transfer chickpeas to a pot filled with water, add baking soda and soak overnight. The next day, discard the water and fill the pot with fresh water, cook a minimum of 4 hours to get soft and puffy chickpeas. Drain water, but reserve 1 cup of the cooked water just in case for later. Take out 2 table-spoons of cooked chickpeas and reserve for decoration, set aside. Transfer cooked chickpeas and all other ingredients except decoration ingredients to a food processor. Mix on high speed for about 5 minutes, scrape the mixer bowl to blend in the mixture and mix again on high speed for about 7-10 minutes. The more you mix the smoother the spread will become. Taste to check flavor, if the hummus is way too thick add 1 tablespoon of the cooked water at a time. Hummus tends to Thicken a little the next day. Transfer to a container or a flat plate, decorate with your choice of decoration, refrigerate immediately, serve cold.

BOREKAS MUSHROOMS ONION 🍎—VEGETARIAN

2 medium onions, chopped small
14 ounces mushrooms, thinly sliced
1/2 teaspoon salt
1/2 teaspoon white pepper
1/2 teaspoon chicken consume powder
1/4 teaspoon turmeric
puff pastry dough, thawed, but very cold
egg for brushing

2 tablespoons sesame seeds
2-3 tablespoons vegetable oil

Preheat oven to 350F (180C), add oil to the pan, add onions, and cook to a light brown color. Now add mushrooms and spices, cook 5 more minutes while mixing. Transfer to a paper towel or colander to rid of oils. Open puff pastry package and roll out, use rolling pin to stretch dough to a 10"x12" sheet. Use a sharp knife to slice dough to get 12 equal squares. Cover squares with clean towel while working on individual bourkas. Scoop out 1 tablespoon of the mushroom mixture and add to the first square, bring top corner to the other facing corner to create a triangle, use a fork to glue the 2 pieces of dough together, it will create a strip like look on the triangle edges. Brush triangle with egg, sprinkle a few sesame seeds and transfer to a foil-lined baking pan. Cover with a clean towel, repeat with the rest of the squares. Bake until puffed and golden brown, about 35-50 minutes. This recipe can also be made as a roulade instead of individual triangles, served warm and crispy.

BOREKAS POTATO AND CARAMELIZED ONIONS ⏰—QUICK & EASY

2 large potatoes, cooked and mashed
2 large onions, chopped small
2-3 tablespoons vegetable oil
1 egg
1/2 teaspoon turmeric
1/2-3/4 teaspoon salt
1/2 teaspoon white pepper
1 package puff pastry, thawed but very cold
1 egg for brushing
2 tablespoons sesame seeds, for decoration

Preheat oven to 350F (180C), add oil and chopped onions to a frying pan, cook to brown onions. Transfer to a colander or paper towel to rid of excess oil. While onions are draining, add potatoes to a large bowl, add egg, turmeric, salt and pepper and mix well. Now add cooked onions and mix well. Open puff pastry dough and use rolling pin to create a 10"x12" sheet and cover dough with a clean towel. Use a sharp knife to divide dough into 12 equal squares. Scoop out 1 tablespoon of the potato mix to add to 1 square of dough. Take 1 corner of the square and pull it toward the facing corner to create a triangle, use a fork to tie them together to form a triangle. Brush Borekas with an egg and sprinkle a few sesame seeds on top. Transfer to a foil-lined baking pan and cover with a clean towel. Repeat with the rest of the squares. Bake for 40-50 minutes or until golden brown. This Borekas can also be shaped as a roulade. Serve warmly.

CLASSIC GREEK TOMATO SAUCE — GREECE ⏰—QUICK & EASY

1 medium onion, grated
2 large garlic cloves, minced
1/4-1/3 cup extra virgin/cold press olive oil
2 pounds fresh tomatoes, peeled and thinly diced
1 tablespoon vinegar
1/2 teaspoon salt
1/2 teaspoon pepper
1/2 cup fresh parsley, leaves only

Heat olive oil in a small pot, add garlic and onion. Cook for 4-5 minutes. Add tomatoes and vinegar, mix well. Add salt and pepper, cover the pot and lower the heat, cook on low for a while, until sauce thickens a little. Add fresh parsley and mix well. Transfer to a glass jar and top with a layer of olive oil. This is a great match for every pasta dish and fish dish, even try it with meat dishes. Store in the refrigerator.

EVERY PARTY'S FAVORITE BOREKITOS PIE — GREEK, SPAIN 🍎 —VEGETARIAN

For the dough—
4 cups flour
1 tablespoon baking powder
2 sticks minus 2 tablespoons salted butter
1 cup sour cream
1/2-2/3 cup cold water
1 teaspoon salt

For the filling—
1 1/2 cups feta cheese
2 cups mozzarella
1/4 cup fresh mixed herbs such as dill, oregano, thyme
1 egg for brushing
2-3 tablespoons sesame seeds to sprinkle

Preheat oven to 375F (190C). Make the dough—Mix all dough ingredients except the salt, knead for about 3-4 minutes then add the salt, now knead for 10 minutes. Wrap in clear plastic and refrigerate for 30 minutes. In a large bowl mix all filling ingredients and set aside. Roll to open the dough, dough should be about 1/4" thick, use a cup to create circles in the dough. Add 1-2 tablespoons of cheese filling to each circle, fold a little, like a 1/2 moon shape to create kind of a "Taco" shape and place with cheese side open in a round baking pan. Repeat with all circles and cheese to create a cake of many half-moons folded in a circle. The circles should not overlap with each other but should be next to each other. Brush top surface with egg and sprinkle with optional sesame seed. Bake until golden brown, serve warm and crispy.

IS IT THAT EASY? PASTEL — MOROCCO 🍎 —VEGETARIAN

2 large potatoes, cooked and mashed
1 egg
1/2 teaspoon salt
1/4 teaspoon black pepper
1/2 teaspoon turmeric
1 large onion chopped small
2 tablespoons vegetable oil plus extra for frying
1 cup warm water and pastry brush
1 package of filo dough or 1 bag egg roll wraps.

Mix the first 5 ingredients and set aside. Cook onion with 2 tablespoons oil until brown. Mix cooked onions with the potato mixture, cut egg roll wraps into 3" by 6" pieces, brush with very little warm water, add 1 tablespoon of potato filling on the egg roll rectangle, start folding 1 corner to create a triangle and keep folding into the next triangle until you reach the end, fold the end into the last triangle pocket. Warm vegetable oil to medium high in frying pan, transfer first 3 pastels to frying pan and fry until they turn golden brown, about 3 minutes, flip pastels to the other side and cook 1-2 more minutes, transfer to a colander or paper towel to drain excess oil. Repeat with the rest of the pastels, serve warm. Pastels can be baked at 350F (180C) if dough is brushed with butter or oil before adding filling.

JERUSELEMITE CLASSIC — EIN KEREM HUMMUS — ISRAEL ⏰ —QUICK & EASY

2 cups dry chickpeas/garbanzo beans
1-1 1/2 teaspoons salt
1/2 teaspoon baking soda
1 cup hummus cooking water

1/2 fresh jalapeño pepper
1/2 bunch fresh parsley, leaves only
1 cup raw tahini (not roasted sesame seed)
juice of 2 lemons
4-5 garlic cloves
1/4 teaspoon ground cumin
2 tablespoons extra virgin olive oil
1/4 teaspoon paprika for garnish

You would be surprised how delicious this Hummus is. Soak chickpeas and baking soda in pot filled with water overnight, the next day dump the water and fill up the pot with fresh water again. Bring the water to a boil, lower the heat and cook chickpeas for 4-6 hours. The chickpeas should be soft and fluffy at this stage. Save at least 1 cup of the cooked water and dump the rest. Place chickpeas, garlic, parsley leaves, and jalapeño pepper in a food processor, now add 1/4 cup of the chickpeas cooked water. Mix the chickpeas mixture for 2-3 minutes, scrape sides of the mixing bowl and grind again for another 2 minutes. Add Tahini, salt, cumin, and lemon juice to the chickpea mixture and grind for another 3-4 minutes. Open the food processor and scrape the side of the mixing bowl again to help all ingredients blend in, grind for another 2 minutes. The spread should be smooth but a little grainy as well, that is normal for this hummus. Taste to correct salt and flavor. Transfer to a container or a serving plate, garnish with a few parsley leaves, paprika and drizzle olive oil. Serve cold, refrigerate extra.

MAMA'S ROSH HASHANA SWEET AND SAVORY PASTELIKOS — MOROCCO ⭐—SPECIALTY

1 large onion thinly chopped
1 1/2 pounds ground beef
1/4 teaspoon nutmeg

1/2 teaspoon ground cloves
1/2 teaspoon cinnamon
1/4 teaspoon salt
1/4 teaspoon white pepper
1/2 cup walnuts or almonds chopped small (optional)
2 tablespoons honey
2 large apples, cubed small
1 packet filo dough
vegetable oil for brushing
2 tablespoons honey for brushing

Preheat oven to 350F (180C). Place chopped onion in a pan with 2 tablespoons vegetable oil, cook to a light brown color. Add ground beef, all spices, honey, and apples, cook for 5-7 minutes to brown the meat. Transfer to a colander or paper towel to drain excess oil. Let meat sit for 15 minutes to cool down, open filo packet, and use scissors to cut squares in size 6.5"x5.5". Cover all filo squares with a clean towel to make sure filo dough doesn't dry out. Take out 1 filo square and brush with very little oil, now add 1 tablespoon of meat filling, pull 1 corner of the square to the other corner to create a triangle, keep folding in a triangle shape until there is no more filo dough to fold, insert extra filo dough inside the last triangle to secure the meat from leaking. Brush the outer side of triangle with very little oil as well, repeat with all filo squares, these pastelikos can be baked or fried, you choose. When pastelikos come out of the oven brush them with a little honey while they are still hot. Serve warmly.

MAMA'S SACHKAH, CHILI SPREAD/PASTE — MOROCCO, TUNISIA, ALGERIA, EGYPT, LEBANON 🌶—HOT & SPICY

4 dried ancho chili pepper
2 teaspoons ground cumin

2-3 garlic cloves, peeled
1 teaspoon caraway seed, toasted and ground
1 teaspoon salt
1 teaspoon cayenne pepper
1/4 cup olive oil
juice of 1/2 lemon

Soak ancho chili peppers in hot water for 1 hour, transfer to a colander to drain excess liquids. Let sit for 15 minutes, add peppers and all ingredients to food processor and process for 3-4 minutes, scrape side of the bowl to mix well and process again for another 5 minutes. Transfer to a glass container and add extra oil. Keep at room temperature, but make sure that it is always covered with a thin layer of olive oil to serve as an oxygen barrier.

MEGINA OR MECHAMER, VEGETABLES PIE NOT TO SKIP — MOROCCO 🌺—IN MEMORY

2 potatoes, peeled, cooked, mashed

8-9 eggs

1 cup frozen peas

1 cup frozen carrots

1/4 cup fresh parsley, chopped

1/2 teaspoon ground turmeric

1/2 teaspoon white pepper

1 teaspoon salt

1/2 teaspoon baking soda
juice of 1/2 lemon
zest of 1/2 lemon

Meat if using —
1 1/2 cups of ground meat
1/2 teaspoon salt
1/2 teaspoon Ras Al Hanut spice mix (see recipe in This & That category)

My nonstick formula for baking (see recipe in this and that category)

Preheat oven to 350F (180C). In a small bowl use a fork to mix all eggs, mash the potatoes and add to eggs. Add all other ingredients in a large bowl. Fold in to mix all ingredients including eggs. If using meat don't add it yet. Brush a round baking pan with my nonstick formula mixture then pour in all the potato eggs mixture. If you are using meat, mix all meat ingredients together and form small balls, arrange meatballs in the potato batter and let them sink in. Bake Magina until the top surface is golden brown, about 45-50 minutes. Squeeze a few lemons juice drops before serving, serve warm or cold.

MOUTHWATERING! MY MAMA'S BEST! CRISPY MEAT CIGARS — MOROCCO ⭐—SPECIALTY

2 tablespoons sweet paprika

1 teaspoon cayenne pepper (optional)

3/4 teaspoon salt

2 tablespoons cumin

12 garlic cloves

20 ounces (700 grams) ground beef

2 large bunches of Italian parsley, leaves only, chopped small

1 package of filo dough

vegetable oil for frying

Mix the first 6 ingredients, transfer to a food processor and grind to a pâté consistency. Transfer meat mixture to a large bowl, add chopped parsley, mix well, refrigerate for 30 minutes. Use scissors to cut out filo dough to 6.5" x 5.5" squares. Filo dough must be covered with a towel to make sure it does not dry out. Add 1 tablespoon of meat filling to filo dough and spread evenly on 1 side of filo dough, fold in 2 outer sides of dough to protect meat from leaking out, then roll filo dough like an egg roll, set on a baking pan then cover cigar with towel to make sure dough does not dry out. Once all cigars have been folded start frying. Heat up oil to medium and add 2 cigars at a time to the hot oil, you might have to put a fork on the cigar to hold it still for the first minute of frying so that they don't open in the hot oil, when the cigar is shaped, it will stay closed in the oil. Fry cigars for 1-2 minutes only, turn to the other side for another minute then transfer to a paper towel or colander to drain excess oil. Serve warm and crispy.

SAMBUSAK OR SAMOSA, O, YUMMY — INDIA ⭐—SPECIALTY

For the dough—
2 1/4 cups flour
1 cup water
1/4 teaspoon baking powder
2 tablespoons butter or olive oil
1/2 teaspoon salt

For the filling—
6 tablespoons vegetable oil

1 large onion chopped small

8 ounces ground meat

1 teaspoon garam masala spice mix (see recipe in This & That category)

1/2 teaspoon ginger, minced or dry powder

1/2 teaspoon chili flaxes or paprika

2 tablespoons lemon juice

1/4 cup cilantro, chopped

1/2 teaspoon each salt and pepper

1 egg for brushing

Preheat oven to 350F (180C). In a mixer place all dough ingredients except the salt, knead for 3-4 minutes, add salt and knead the dough until it's elastic and soft to touch. Wrap dough with a towel and let rest for 30 minutes at room temperature. Make the filling—add onion to a pan with oil, cook for 5 minutes to brown a little, add meat and all other filling ingredients. Cook to brown the meat, mix consistently. Transfer filling to a colander to drain excess oil, let cool down. Roll dough to open, use rolling pin to make dough a 1/4" thick and place a cup on dough to create a circle. Place 2 tablespoons on the dough and fold circle into a half-moon shape, use a fork to glue the 2 sides of dough. Brush samosa with an egg and transfer to a foil-lined baking pan. Repeat with all dough circles. Bake until golden brown, about 25-30 minutes, serve warm.

SPINACH CHEESE BOREKAS FOR EVERY OCCASION — GREEK 🍎—VEGETARIAN

1 bag frozen spinach

2 medium onions, chopped small

1 pound mozzarella shredded

1/2 teaspoon each salt and pepper

1/4 teaspoon nutmeg

1 package puff pastry thawed but cold
1 egg for brushing
2 tablespoons sesame seeds to sprinkle
2 tablespoons vegetable oil for spinach
3 tablespoons vegetable oil to brown onions

Preheat oven to 350F. In a pan add 2 tablespoons oil and add spinach, cook while mixing for 5 minutes on medium heat, just enough to thaw. Transfer spinach to a bowl, let cool. In the same pan add 3 tablespoons oil and onions and cook to brown, set aside to drain excess oil. When the spinach cools down, squeeze some of its liquid, now add the onions, cheese and spices, mix well. Open puff pastry and use a roller to stretch it into a large rectangle 12"x10", add the spinach mixture to the very top part of the 10", set the filling like a log, and fold in the 2 outside dough sides to block filling from leaking out. Start rolling the dough to form a roulade, but don't roll it too tight, leave some air between to let dough rise. Place on a foil-lined baking pan with the seam facing down to help secure the folded roulade. Brush with egg, sprinkle sesame seeds on top, bake until golden brown about 40-50 minutes. This appetizer is also great as an individual triangle or samosa half-moon shape, serve warm.

WELCOME THE NEXT GUEST WITH VEGETARIAN CHOPPED LIVER 🍎—VEGETARIAN

2 large eggplants, cubed small
3 tablespoons vegetable or walnut oil
3 large onions, chopped small
2-3 tablespoons vegetable oil
5 hardboiled eggs, sliced
1/2 teaspoon each salt and black pepper
1/4 teaspoon salt (add later after final tasting)

1 cup walnuts

Preheat oven to 400F (200C). Place cubed eggplants in a foil-lined baking pan, drizzle 3 tablespoons oil, mix oil and eggplant well, transfer to the oven, bake for 25 minutes. Place onions in a pan, add 2-3 tablespoons oil and cook to brown. Transfer all ingredients to food processor and grind for 3-5 minutes, scrape the sides of the mixing bowl and grind another 3-5 minutes to get a smooth spread. Taste to see if the spread needs extra salt. Transfer to a container and refrigerate. This spread is great when served with onion jam, serve cold.

YAFFA'S AVOCADO BAKED (OR FRIED) EGG ROLLS 🍎 — VEGETARIAN

1 ripe avocado, mashed
2 green onions thinly chopped
1 carrot thinly shredded
1 teaspoon fresh minced ginger root
1/2 teaspoon salt
1/4 teaspoon white pepper
1 teaspoon fresh lemon zest
1/4 cup chopped fresh cilantro
1/4 cup freshly squeezed lemon juice
1 egg for brushing
1 bag of egg roll wraps
Optional—1/4 preserved lemon, chopped small

Ginger, cilantro and lemon, you can't go wrong with this combination. I fell in love with a similar dish in a restaurant and it inspired me to create this delicious recipe. Turn on oven to 350F (180C), mix all ingredients except the egg roll wraps in a large bowl, measure 2 tablespoons of the mixture and transfer onto 1 egg roll wrap, fold in 2 outer sides, roll the avocado filling like an egg roll, brush top with egg. Line a baking pan with foil, transfer the avocado egg rolls to the baking pan, bake for 30 minutes or until the egg rolls are light brown color. One recipe filling yield 5 Avocado egg rolls.

YAFFA'S OWN CRISPY ASPARAGUS IN TWISTED PASTRY ⏰— QUICK & EASY

1 pound fresh asparagus
1/2 teaspoon salt
1 package puff pastry
1 egg for brushing
2 tablespoons sesame seeds

Preheat oven to 350F (180C). Fill up a pot large enough to fit the asparagus with water and bring to a boil, place asparagus in the boiling water and cook 5 minutes only. Transfer asparagus to a clean towel or paper towel and let cool down for 10 minutes. Open puff pastry package and use scissors to cut a size of 2" x 6" each. Take 1 piece of puff pastry and roll it to a thin log, wrap the pastry log onto the asparagus in circle motions while covering all the length of the edible part of asparagus. Transfer wrapped asparagus to a foil-lined baking pan, brush with egg and sprinkle a few sesame seeds along the twisted puff pastry. Bake until golden brown, serve warm and crispy.

YAFFA'S OWN GF CREPES STUFFED WITH MUSHROOMS AND CARAMELIZED ONION ⭐—SPECIALTY

1 tablespoon chia seeds or flax seeds for binding
2 tablespoons vegetable oil
1 medium potato, peeled, cooked, mashed
1 large onion, chopped small
3-4 eggs
1/4 teaspoon each salt and pepper
2 cups mushrooms, thinly sliced

Place chia or flax seeds in a small bowl with 3 tablespoons water, let it sit for at least 5 minutes. In a food processor place the potato, eggs, chia seeds, salt, and pepper, mix for a few minutes to get a smooth batter. Set aside to settle. Add oil to a pan with the onion, cook to brown and add mushrooms, salt and pepper cook another 5 minutes, transfer to a colander to drain excess oils and cool down.

Cook the crepes—warm 2 tablespoons oil in a pan, scoop out 1 soup ladle and add to the pan, make sure that the heat is no more than medium. Cook 2-3 minutes on 1 side just until you see a few brown spots, flip to the other side, cook for another minute, transfer to a plate, let cool down. Scoop out 2 tablespoons of mushroom filling and line up on 1 crepe, fold in the 2 outer sides, then roll the crepe into a log. Serve warm.

YAFFA'S OWN — MIDDLE EAST MEETS FAR-EAST CHICKEN EGG ROLLS ⭐—SPECIALTY

Make the marinade first—
1 tablespoon soy sauce
1 tablespoon dry white wine
1 tablespoon flour or cornstarch
1/2 teaspoon sugar
1/2 teaspoon ginger, minced

For the egg roll filling—
1 onion, chopped small
2 pounds chicken meat, breast or dark, chopped small
1 cup fresh sprouts, chopped
3 fresh celery sticks, chopped small
1/4 fresh green cabbage, chopped small
1 fresh carrot, shredded
2 teaspoons curry powder
1/2 teaspoon salt
2 tablespoons flour or cornstarch
1-2 bags egg roll wraps or small 8" tortilla
oil for brushing

Preheat oven to 350F (180C). Mix all marinade ingredients and set aside. Cut chicken meat into very small pieces and transfer to marinade, mix well, refrigerate for 30 minutes. Add 2 tablespoons oil to a pan and add onion, cook to lightly brown, now add the rest of the vegetables and spices, cook stir fry for 5 minutes before adding the chicken, mix well and cook for another 5 minutes. Let cool down a little. Brush 1 egg roll or tortilla with very little oil, add 2-3 tablespoon of the chicken filling to the egg roll. Fold in the 2 outer sides to secure the filling from leaking, fold to roll the front edge and roll until there is no more egg roll dough to roll. Brush the outer side of the egg roll with a little oil and place on a foil-lined baking pan. If frying, hold the egg roll with seam down for the first minute, if baking, brush with egg, transfer to oven and bake until golden brown, serve warm.

YAFFA'S SAVORY FAVORITE — PORTABELLO VENETSIA ⭐ — SPECIALTY

4 large fresh portobello mushrooms, washed, drained
1 cup goat cheese
1 recipe of Yaffa's restaurant's favorite main dish marinade (see recipe in This & That category)

In my previous restaurant this was a favorite. Preheat the oven to 425F (218C). Place the portobello mushrooms in a baking pan lined with foil, bake for 5 minutes. There are 2 options for this unique recipe. First option—drizzle 3 tablespoons of the main dish marinade on the mushroom before the baking and bake for about 10 minutes, serve from the oven. Second option—bake the portobello mushroom for 4-5 minutes, take out, add a layer of goat cheese on top of the portobello, then drizzle 2-3 tablespoons of the main dish marinade, return to the oven for another 5-6 minutes, serve warm from the oven with crispy bread. This recipe yields 4 vegetarian main dishes or split to halves to get 8 vegetables side dish.

YAFFA'S SAVORY MEAT AND HARISSA BOREKAS

1 large onion, chopped small
2-3 tablespoons vegetable oil
1 1/2 pounds ground beef
3-4 garlic cloves minced
1 teaspoon sweet paprika

1/2 teaspoon black pepper

1 teaspoon cumin

1/2 teaspoon turmeric

2 tablespoons Harissa (see recipe in This & That category)

1 package puff pastry dough

1 egg for brushing

2 tablespoons sesame seeds to sprinkle

Preheat oven to 350F (180C). Add oil and onions to pan, cook to golden brown. Add ground beef, minced garlic, all the spices, and Harissa to a pan and cook meat until brown while mixing constantly. Transfer to a colander or paper towel to drain excess oils and liquids. Open puff pastry dough and roll out with a roller pin to create a 10" x12" sheet. Divide dough into 12 equal squares, cover with a clean towel. Scoop out 1 tablespoon of meat mixture and place on 1 square of dough, pull out top corner of the square to the corner facing it on the other side to create a triangle. Use a fork to tie the 2 sides together, brush triangle with egg and sprinkle sesame seeds, transfer to a foil-lined baking pan and cover with clean towel. Repeat with the rest of the squares. Remove towel before baking. Bake for 40-50 minutes until golden brown, serve warm and crispy.

YAFFA'S SAVORY, TASTY, CRISPY HAMANTASCHEN 🍎— VEGETARIAN

For the dough—

2 egg yolks (reserve egg whites for brushing)

2 sticks salted butter, shredded

2 cups all-purpose flour

1/2 teaspoon baking powder

1/2 teaspoon salt

For the filling—
1 large onion chopped small
2 tablespoons olive oil
1/2 teaspoon white pepper
1/4 teaspoon turmeric
1 teaspoon chicken consume powder
2 tablespoons sesame seeds to sprinkle
8 ounces mushrooms, thinly sliced

Preheat oven to 400F (200C). In a mixer place the first 4 dough ingredients, mix for 5 minutes then add salt, if the dough seems dry add 1-2 tablespoons cold water, mix well to get a soft dough. Wrap in clear plastic wrap and refrigerate for 30 minutes. Make the filling by adding oil to a pan then add onions and brown, add mushrooms and all spices and cook 5 minutes, drain on paper towel or a colander for 10 minutes to rid of excess oil. Roll dough to open, dough should be about 1/4" think, use a cup and a butter knife to create circles of dough, scoop out 2 tablespoon of mushrooms filling and place on 1 circle of dough, pinch dough on 2 sides than pinch third side to create a triangle shape. Brush with egg white and sprinkle a few sesame seeds on top. Repeat with all the other circles of dough. Bake for 25-35 minutes, serve warm and crispy.

Soups
& Salads

HELPFUL HINTS

- If the soup is not intended as the main course, count on 1 quart to serve 6. As the main dish, plan on 1 quart to serve 2.
- After cooking vegetables, pour any water and leftover vegetable pieces into a freezer container. When full, add tomato juice and seasoning to create a money saving "free soup".
- Instant potatoes help thicken soups and stews.
- A leaf of lettuce dropped in a pot of soup absorbs grease from the top—remove the lettuce and serve. You can also make soup the day before, chill, and scrape off the hardened fat that rises to the top.
- To cut down on odors when cooking cabbage or cauliflower, add a little vinegar to the water and don't overcook.
- Three large stalks of celery, chipped and added to about 2 cups of beans (navy, brown, pinto, etc.), make the dish easier to digest.
- Fresh is best, but to reduce time in the kitchen, use canned or frozen broths or bouillon bases. Canned or frozen

vegetables, such as peas, green beans, and corn, also work well.

- Ideally, cold soups should be served in chilled bowls.
- Perk up soggy lettuce by spritzing it with a mixture of lemon juice and cold water.
- You can easily remove eggshells from hard-boiled eggs if you quickly rinse the eggs in cold water after they are boiled. Add a drop of food coloring to help distinguish cooked eggs from raw ones.
- Your fruit salads will look better when you use an egg slicer to make perfect slices of strawberries, kiwis, or bananas.
- The ratio for a vinaigrette is typically 3 parts oil to 1 part vinegar.
- For salads, cook pasta al dente (slightly chewy to the bite). This allows the pasta to absorb some of the dressing and not become mushy.
- Fresh vegetables require little seasoning or cooking. If the vegetable is old, dress it up with sauces and seasonings.
- Chill the serving plates to keep the salad crisp.
- Fruit juices, such as pineapple and orange, can be used as salad dressing by adding a little olive oil, nutmeg, and honey.

A FANCY SHMANCY LETTUCE SALAD? QUICK & EASY ⏰— QUICK & EASY

2 large heads of romaine lettuce, washed
4 large celery sticks, cubed small, washed
1/2 teaspoon each salt and white pepper
2 small garlic cloves, minced
1 tablespoon mustard
2-3 tablespoons olive oil

Make the marinade first, in a mixing bowl place salt, white pepper, minced garlic, mustard, and olive oil, mix to blend and set aside. Use a cutting board and a sharp knife to chop the lettuce, transfer the lettuce and chopped celery to the marinade bowl, fold in to blend with the marinade. Refrigerate until ready to serve. Serve cold.

BEST EVER TASTY TOMATO SOUP ⏰—QUICK & EASY

2-3 tablespoons olive oil
1 onion, chopped
1 leek, white part only, chopped
3 medium carrots cubed
4-6 garlic cloves, crushed
2 sweet potatoes, cubed
8-9 fresh tomatoes, crushed
3 tablespoons tomato paste
1 tablespoon sugar
8-10 cups water
1 cup fresh basil, chopped
1/4 cup fresh cilantro, chopped

Heat oil in a large pot and cook onion, add leek, carrots, and garlic, cook 3 minutes while mixing. Add sweet potatoes, tomatoes, tomato paste, sugar, salt, pepper, and water, bring to a boil, lower heat and cook 30 minutes. Use a food processor or a blender to ground to a paste consistency, add both herbs and cook another 5 minutes. Let sit for 15 minutes for the flavors to blend. Serve hot with fresh, crispy bread.

CHEF YAFFA'S DIVINE BEET CARPACCIO ⭐—SPECIALTY

3 large beets, cooked, peeled, thinly sliced
1 cup feta cheese or goat cheese, crumbled
1/4 cup cherry tomatoes, sliced
1/4 cup fresh Italian parsley, chopped, leaves only
1 1/2 teaspoons cumin
1/2-1 cup walnuts or pecans, chopped
1/4 cup olive oil
1/2 teaspoon salt
1/2 teaspoon white pepper
1/3 cup white vinegar

Make the marinade first, add vinegar, salt, white pepper, olive oil, walnuts, cumin, and Italian parsley to a mixing bowl, mix well, set aside. Choose the serving plate that the beet carpaccio will be served, set the beet slices on the whole tray going around in circles. Arrange the half sliced cherry tomatoes on the beet slices, sprinkle the Feta cheese or goat cheese crumbles all over the beet slices, drizzle the marinade all over the beet slices, make sure each beet slice gets a little of the flavored marinade. Cover with a clear plastic and refrigerate for an hour before serving for the flavors to blend. Serve cold.

CLASSIC VILLAGE STYLE SALAD — GREEK 🍎—VEGETARIAN

3 fresh tomatoes, 1" cubed
1 fresh cucumber 1/2" cubed
1 yellow or purple onion, sliced in rings
1 fresh hot green pepper, sliced in rings (optional)
1/2 cup black or kalamata olives
8 ounces sheep's cheese
1-2 hardboiled eggs
1/4 cup extra virgin/cold press olive oil
2 tablespoons white vinegar
1/2 teaspoon oregano
1-2 teaspoons capers
1/4-1/2 teaspoon ground pepper
salt, only add after final tasting

Make marinade first, in a mixing bowl add olive oil, vinegar, oregano, and black pepper and mix well. Place all fresh vegetables, olives, capers, and eggs, gently fold in to mix. Sprinkle the cheese on top or serve the cheese in slices and refrigerate until serving. Serve cold with freshly baked crispy bread.

CLASSIC YEMENITE MEAT SOUP — YEMEN 🍲—SLOW COOKER

4 pounds beef meat for stew, cubed
4 beef bones
2-3 medium onions, chopped small

10 garlic cloves, sliced

1/2 teaspoon each salt and pepper

4-5 cardamon pods

1 tablespoon ground cumin

1 tablespoon Turmeric

2 tablespoons Hawayage for soup (middle east spice mix, can be purchased here— https://amazon.com/shop/sephardicflavors)

9 ounces tomato paste

1 zucchini, cubed

1 carrot, cubed

2 fresh tomatoes, cubed

1 bunch fresh cilantro, chopped

7 small potatoes, cubed large

This is a large soup. Fill up a large pot with about 15-22 cups water, add all meat and bones for 20 minutes, add onions, garlic, and tomato paste, and cook for 1.5 hours. Add all other ingredients except the potatoes, cover, cook/simmer for 5 hours on low heat until meat is very soft, 40 minutes before end of cooking add the potatoes. Serve hot with spicy hot Schug and fresh, crispy bread.

EASY AND HEARTWARMING VEGETARIAN WINTER SOUP — ISRAEL 🍎—VEGETARIAN

1 large onion, chopped

2 tablespoons vegetable oil

5-6 garlic cloves, sliced

3 carrots, cubed

1.5 fresh kohlrabi, cubed

2 potatoes, cubed

1 parsnip root, cubed small

1 squash cubed

4 celery sticks, chopped
1/2-2/3 cup orange lentils
1 cup garbanzo beans, cooked
1 tablespoon onion soup powder or kosher parve chicken consume, (it is vegetarian)
1/4 teaspoon each salt and pepper
1/2 teaspoon turmeric
1/2-1/3 celery root, cubed
12-13 cup water
Optional—2 cups pasta vermicelli

Heat a pot with oil, add onions, cook 3-5 minutes, add garlic, cook another 2 minutes, add all vegetables, water and spices, bring to a boil, cover and lower the heat, cook for about 1-1.5 hours. If you choose to add the pasta, add it in the last 30 minutes. Serve hot and let cool completely before refrigeration.

GONDI — A CELEBRATION OF A CLASSIC PERSIAN SOUP - IRAN ◉—SLOW COOKER

2 large chicken thighs
1 cup chickpeas, soaked in water overnight
2 zucchinis, sliced 1"
2 dry lemons, Persian style (can be found in Mediterranean/Middle East stores)
1/2 teaspoon turmeric

For the chicken balls—
1 pound chicken breast, ground
3 medium onions, thinly shredded
1 cup chickpeas flour
1/4 cup vegetable oil

1 teaspoon ground cardamom

1 teaspoon cumin

1 teaspoon turmeric

1/2-1 teaspoon salt

1/4-1/2 teaspoon white pepper

1/4-1/2 cup water as needed

Cook the chickpeas for 1 hour with water, discard the water, in a large pot add chicken thighs, chickpeas, zucchini, Persian dry lemons, turmeric, and 1/4 teaspoon salt, add about 10 cups water, bring to a boil, lower the heat, cover and cook for 1 hour. While the soup is cooking, make the "Gondi" balls, mix all ingredients for the chicken balls, wet your hands to prevent filling from sticking, form small balls about 2/3" in size, add chicken balls to the boiling soup, cook about an hour in a partially covered pot. Serve hot.

HEAVENLY TASTY CARROT SALAD — MOROCCO ⭐—SPECIALTY

4-6 fresh garlic cloves, minced

1 teaspoon cumin

2-3 tablespoons Harissa (see recipe in This & That category)

Juice of 2 lemons or 1/3 cup of white vinegar

1/4 cup olive oil

1/2 cup chopped Italian parsley, leaves only

1/2 teaspoon salt

1/4 teaspoon black pepper

2.2 pounds fresh carrots, peeled

Make the marinade first—in a mixing bowl place all ingredients except the carrots, mix well and let sit for 30 minutes. While the marinade's flavors are getting infused, cook the carrots, bring a large pot of water to a boil, cut carrots to a size of 1/2" and transfer to the boiling water, cook for about 15-20 minutes, carrots should be half cooked, drain all water and add carrots to the marinade bowl, mix well, cover bowl with a clear plastic and refrigerate for minimum 1 hour before serving, this salad tastes even better the next day. Serve cold, refrigerate extra salad.

HERE COMES THE BABA GANUSH SPREAD/DIP 🍎— VEGETARIAN

2 fresh eggplants

6 small garlic cloves, peeled

1/2 cup raw Tahini

1/2 cup lemon juice

1 teaspoon olive oil

1/2 teaspoon salt

1/2 cup fresh Italian parsley, leaves only, for decoration

Preheat oven to broil, make 5-6 small slits in the eggplants, insert garlic in each slit and place on a foil-lined baking pan and transfer to the oven. Broil eggplants for about 7 minutes on each side, it should start burning a little, which is what we want. This is what creates the smoky flavor. Depending on your oven you might need a little more broiling time. When eggplant is charred 1/3 way, take it out and let it cool down as is. Use a serrated knife to slice eggplant and open with the inside filling facing out. Use a spoon to scoop out all the "meat" and transfer to a colander to drain excess liquids, keep in colander for 5 minutes, set aside. In a food processor add all other ingredients except the parsley, mix on high for 3 minutes, scrape and taste to see if it needs more salt or lemon juice, mix again for another few minutes. Add eggplants to the food processor and pulse only 2 times, 3 seconds each time, open and check consistency, it might not need more mixing. Baba Ganush should be coarse chunks, not creamy. You might need another pulse. You can also just mash the eggplant with a fork. Transfer to a container and refrigerate. Baba Ganush is good for several days, served chilled with pita bread or crackers.

MAMA'S BEST SEPHARDIC BEET SALAD — MOROCCO ⭐— SPECIALTY

2.2 pounds fresh beets
2 fresh lemons or 1/4 cup white vinegar
1 1/2 cups fresh Italian parsley, leaves only, chopped
1/4 cup olive oil
1/4 teaspoon black pepper
1/2-1 teaspoon salt
1 1/2-2 teaspoons cumin

Make the marinade first, add all ingredients except the beets to a mixing bowl and mix well, set aside. Place beets in a pot and fill up the pot with water and cook for 30-40 minutes until the beets are soft and the peel comes off easily, transfer to a colander to drain the water and cool down. Use your fingers to remove the skin, cut the leaves and set aside, they can be added to the salad as well, cube the beets to a size of 1/2" each and chop the leaves as well, add the chopped beets and leaves to the marinade and fold in to mix well. Transfer to a container and refrigerate. Serve chilled.

MAMA'S "CHSHU" HEARTWARMING WINTER SEMOLINA SOUP — MOROCCO 🌺—IN MEMORY

3 tablespoons vegetable oil
3 large onions, chopped small
1 cup fresh cilantro, chopped
1 cup fresh celery, chopped
2 large tomatoes, shredded
1/2 teaspoon white pepper
1/2-1 teaspoon salt
1/2 teaspoon turmeric
10 cups water
3/4 cup semolina

Heat up oil, add onions, cook 5 minutes, add celery and cilantro, cook to golden brown, add tomatoes and spices, mix well, add water and cook 40 minutes, add semolina and mix constantly while cooking on low heat to make sure that semolina does not stick to the bottom of the pan, cook another 10-15 minutes, serve hot.

MAMA'S SPLIT PEA SOUP — MOROCCO 🟡—SLOW COOKER

1 large onion chopped
3 tablespoons olive oil
1 teaspoon garlic, minced
3 tablespoons cilantro, chopped
1 large carrot, cubed small
2 celery sticks, chopped
1/2 teaspoon cumin

1/4-1/2 teaspoon salt
1 cup dry split peas
1-2 tablespoons fresh parsley, chopped
1 tablespoon kosher parve chicken consume (it is vegetarian)

This recipe was another big hit in my restaurant, so much so that customers used to order it in advance to take an extra one home. Heat oil in a large pot, add onions and garlic, add split peas and water, cover, bring to a boil, lower the heat and cook for 1 hour, add all other ingredients, cover & simmer for another hour. Serve hot with fresh, crispy bread, let cool completely before refrigeration.

MAMA'S "THE SILK SOUP" HARIRAH — MOROCCO 🌺—IN MEMORY

2.2 pounds beef or chicken
3-4 bones, chicken or beef
1 cup brown lentils
1 cup chickpeas, cooked in water
2 cups diced fresh tomatoes
1/2 cup flour (for GF use rice or cornflour)
1/2 cup freshly squeezed lemon juice
16 cup water
1 cup thin pasta such as vermicelli
1 celery root with leaves, cubed
1 bunch fresh Italian parsley, chopped
1 bunch of fresh cilantros, chopped
3 medium onions
1 teaspoon black pepper
1/2 teaspoon turmeric
salt, as needed

Harira soup was served in my restaurant all year long, customers loved the lemony, savory flavor, a truly unique but delicious soup. The word Harira means silk in Moroccan, this is a large soup, if making for less than 4 guests I suggest cutting all ingredients in a half. In a large pot add meat, bones, chickpeas, and lentils. In a small pan, cook the onions to translucent and add to the large pot, add water, tomatoes, celery, and cook for 1.5 hours, mix the flour with 1 cup of cold water to avoid lumps and add to the pot, add the pasta, parsley, cilantro, and continue cooking on low for another 30 minutes. Add the lemon juice, and cook on low another 15 minutes, once the flour is added mix more to make sure that flour does not stick to the bottom of the pot. This soup is very thick and satisfying as a meal. Serve hot.

ONE OF THE CLASSICS — ZAA'LUKA SALAD — MOROCCO

3 medium eggplants washed
2 jalapeño peppers
6-8 garlic cloves
1/4 cup white vinegar
2 cups water
1/2-1 teaspoon ground cumin
1/4 cup olive oil
1 teaspoon sweet paprika
1/2-1 teaspoon salt

Use a sharp paring knife to make a few slits in each eggplant, insert 1 garlic clove and 1/4 jalapeño pepper in each slit, add water to a pot that can fit the eggplants, cover the pot and bring to a boil then reduce the heat and cook for 30 minutes, if the eggplants are not soft enough add another 10-15 minutes to the cooking time. Transfer the eggplants to a colander to drain all water, let the eggplants cool down, slice eggplants to open and scrape the inside content like it is done in the Baba Ganush (see recipe in salads category), discard the skin, transfer content to a mixing bowl, mash eggplants with a fork to get a soft consistency, add cumin, olive oil, paprika, and vinegar and mash while mixing all ingredients together to create a flavorful eggplant salad. Taste to check if salad needs salt, refrigerate, serve chilled.

POMEGRANATE & MEAT SOUP — A PERSIAN CELEBRATION —SLOW COOKER

1/4 cup olive oil
1.5 pounds meat for stew
2 large onions, chopped
5 garlic cloves, sliced
1 cup dry yellow split peas or dry green peas
8 cups boiling water
1 teaspoon crushed chili pepper
2 teaspoons sweet paprika
1 tablespoon turmeric
1 cinnamon stick
1/4 teaspoon fennel seeds ground
1 teaspoon salt
1 teaspoon black pepper
1/4 cup pomegranate syrup
1 tablespoon sugar

For serving—
1 cup of mixed herbs such as mint, cilantro, parsley
1 cup white rice, cooked

In a large pot, heat up the oil and brown the meat, transfer to a plate, add onions to the same pot and brown onions, add yellow peas, mix for 1 minute, add the meat back to the pot and all the other ingredients, cook for about 2 hours. Serve hot accompanied with white rice and herbs.

POPULAR SAFFRON FISH SOUP — TUNISIA, LIBYA ⬤—SLOW COOKER

4 pounds white fish such as Sea Bass or Cod crushed including heads and bones to make fish stock
1/2 cup freshly squeezed lemon juice
6-7 tablespoons olive oil
1 large onion, chopped
7-8 garlic cloves, minced
1 tablespoon sweet paprika
1-2 tablespoons tomato paste
1/2 cup tomatoes, crushed
1/2 red bell pepper, diced
1 bulb fresh fennel, cubed small
1/8 teaspoon saffron threads
1/2-1 teaspoon ground cumin
2/3 cup fresh Italian parsley, chopped
2 cups croutons

Rub fish with salt, pepper, and lemon juice, refrigerate, place fish heads and bones in a stockpot, add water to cover, bring to a boil, lower the heat, cook for 30-40 minutes, discard the fish bones and heads and save the cooked water. Sauté onions and garlic for 2 minutes, add paprika, tomato paste, crashed tomatoes and stir well, add bell pepper, fennel, saffron, cumin, reserved fish stock, and parsley, simmer for 25 minutes, add fish and simmer another 15 minutes, do not overcook the fish, remove fish from the pot. discard parsley. To serve- add broth to a soup plate, place 1 piece of fish on top and sprinkle croutons. Serve warm, this recipe yields about 6-7 servings.

POTATO SOUP CAN BE SO GOOD — MOROCCO, SYRIA 🟡—SLOW COOKER

5-6 Potatoes, cubed, peeled soaked in water
3 Chicken or beef bones
1 pound chicken or beef, cubed
2 tablespoons vegetable oil
1/4 cup fresh cilantro, cubed
1/2 teaspoon white pepper
1/4-1/2 teaspoon turmeric
12-13 cups water
1/2-1 teaspoon salt

Peel the potatoes, slice to halves only, transfer the potatoes to a large pot, add oil and bones, meat and water, bring to a boil, cover and cook on low heat for 20-30 minutes, uncover and mash the potatoes, add all other ingredients and cover again, cook for another 30 minutes on low heat, let cool down and refrigerate. Serve hot.

RIBOLITA TUSCAN FARMERS SOUP — ITALY 🟡—SLOW COOKER

1/4 cup Extra virgin/cold press olive oil
7 ounces butter
2 purple onions, chopped
1 large yellow onion, chopped
4-6 garlic cloves minced
3 fresh carrots, cubed
1 celery root with some green leaves, cubed
Parmesan cheese to sprinkle
1/2 teaspoon lemon zest
2 large potatoes, cubed small
1 cup white beans, already cooked

20 ounces fresh diced tomatoes
1 bunch Swiss chard, chopped small
1 teaspoon fresh rosemary
1/2-1 teaspoon each salt and pepper
slice of crispy bread for each guest

Use a pot that can be transferred to the oven later. Heat up oil and butter in a large pot, add onions, garlic, carrots, celery, lemon zest, and potatoes and cook 25-30 minutes. Add beans, tomatoes, Swiss chard, rosemary, and water, bring to a boil, lower the heat, cover the pot, cook for 2 hours. Add salt and pepper and mix, transfer the pot to an oven and bake for one hour, place one slice of bread in each soup plate, top it with soup, sprinkle with Parmesan cheese, transfer to the oven and bake for 10 minutes, serve hot from the oven with fresh, crispy bread.

SAVORY MEAT & BEANS SOUP — YEMEN ●—SLOW COOKER

3 beef bones
1 pound beef for stew, cubed
2 cups white beans, soaked inwater overnight
2 large onions, chopped
4 garlic cloves, minced
3 large carrots, cubed
5 fresh tomatoes, crushed
1 1/2 tablespoons tomato paste
1 1/4 tablespoons Hawayage (can be ordered from my Mediterranean shop here- https://amazon.com/shop/sephardicflavors))
5-6 large potatoes, cubed large
1/2-1 teaspoon salt

Preheat oven to 420F (200C). Transfer bones to a foil-lined baking pan and brown for 20 minutes. In a large pot add meat and bones with 12 cup water, add all other ingredients except the potatoes, cook on low heat for about 2 hours to soften the beans. Add the potatoes and cook another 40 minutes, taste to see if more salt is needed. Serve hot with Schug (recipe in the This & That category) and crispy bread.

SAVORY SMOKY EGGPLANT SALAD

3 large eggplants
1 fresh head of garlic cloves, sliced and skin peeled off
1/2 preserved lemon, chopped or 2 tablespoons freshly squeezed lemon juice
2-3 tablespoon olive oil
1/2-1 teaspoon salt
1/2 teaspoon pepper

Preheat oven to broil or use a charcoal grill, wash and dry eggplants but keep stems intact, use a sharp paring knife to slice 4 slits in each eggplant, insert one garlic clove in each slit, do the same with all 3 eggplants. Line a baking pan with foil and transfer eggplants to the pan. If using charcoal grill, place eggplant directly on the grill. If using an oven, insert baking pan in the oven and let the eggplant roast well on all sides. The eggplants will release liquids and shrink as well, that is normal, when the eggplants have many dark charcoaled spots on their skin, take them out and let them cool down for 30 minutes. Slice to open one eggplant, and scoop out the inside, transfer to a bowl, repeat with all eggplants, discard the burnt skin. Mash the eggplant "meat" with a fork or a potato masher to get a chunky consistency, add salt, pepper, and preserved lemon or fresh lemon juice, fold in gently to mix, refrigerate until serving, serve chilled.

TUBULE SALAD — LEBANON ⏰ —QUICK & EASY

1 cup Bulgur wheat, cracked wheat for tubule salad
3 bunches of fresh Italian parsley, chopped small
1/2 bunch fresh mint, leaves only, chopped small
1 small onion, yellow or purple, chopped small
1/2 cup extra virgin olive oil
1/2 cup freshly squeezed lemon juice
1/2-1 teaspoon each salt and pepper
1 cup fresh tomato, cubed

Soak the Bulgur Wheat in hot water for one hour. Transfer to a colander to drain all water. Add all ingredients and fold to blend flavors. Chill for 1 hour before serving. This recipe yields about 5-6 servings.

WINTER COMFORT CHICKPEAS SOUP — ISRAEL

4 tablespoons olive oil
2 large onions, chopped
6 ounces smoked beef or smoked turkey
1/2 teaspoon turmeric

2 pounds chickpeas, soaked in water overnight

2 large potatoes, cubed

2 large carrots, cubed

4 celery sticks, chopped

7 cups clear chicken broth

1/2 teaspoon coriander seeds, ground

1/2-1 teaspoon each salt and pepper

Cook the chickpeas first, dump the overnight water, and refill the chickpeas pot with fresh water, cook for 4 hours, dump the chickpeas water or reserve for something else, heat the oil in another pot, add onion and brown for 5 minutes. Add smoked meat and cook for another 5 minutes, add all other ingredients except the salt and bring to a boil. Lower the heat, cover and cook for 30 minutes, check to see if more salt is needed, serve warm, this recipe yields 8 servings.

YAFFA'S CHICKEN SOUP TO TREASURE

1 large onion, chopped small

1 large tomato, shredded

2 teaspoon vegetable oil

1/2 cup fresh dill, chopped

1 cup fresh parsley, chopped

2 zucchinis, cubed 1"

3 carrots, cubed 1/2"

3 celery sticks, cubed 1"

2 pounds whole chicken (no need to cut)

One of these 3 roots—celery root, parsley root, parsnip root, cubed small

1 large potato, cubed

8 cups water

1/2-1 teaspoon each salt and pepper

1 tablespoon chicken consume

Place all ingredients in a large pot except the salt and chicken consume, add 8 cups of water, cover the pot and bring pot to a boil, lower the heat and cook for 30 minutes. Uncover the pot and add the salt and chicken consume, gently mix and cover again. Cook for at least another hour, let cool down, serve warm and store extra in the refrigerator.

CHEF YAFFA'S CHILDHOOD ISRAELI SALAD — ISREAL 🍎— VEGETARIAN

1 fresh green bell pepper, cubed small
1 small cucumber, cubed small
2 fresh tomatoes, cubed small
1 small fresh garlic, minced
2-4 tablespoons extra virgin/cold press olive oil
1/2 teaspoon each salt and pepper
1 tablespoon freshly squeezed lemon juice

Place lemon juice, olive oil, salt, pepper, and garlic in a bowl, mix well, let sit for 5 minutes. Add all cubed vegetables to the bowl and mix well. Serve freshly made salad chilled with crispy bread. Store extra in the refrigerator.

YAFFA'S FARMER MARKETS FALL IN LOVE FAVA BEANS DELIGHT SALAD 🍎—VEGETARIAN

1.5 pounds fresh or frozen fava beans, skin peeled
1/2-1 teaspoon salt
3 garlic cloves, minced
1/2 cup fresh cilantro, leaves and stems, chopped
2-3 tablespoons white vinegar

1 1/2 teaspoons ground cumin
3-4 tablespoons cold press olive oil

Place a large pot of water on the stove and bring to a boil. Add fava beans and salt, cook to soften the beans, about 15- 20 minutes. Transfer to a colander to drain the water. In a mixing bowl add all other ingredients and mix well. Let sit for 30 minutes for the flavors to blend. Gently fold in the fava beans. Refrigerate for 30 minutes, this salad tastes even better the next day, refrigerate extra.

YAFFA'S LEMON GINGER CELERY SALAD ⭐—SPECIALTY

2 tablespoons olive oil
5 fresh garlic cloves, chopped
1 teaspoon fresh ginger, chopped
1/4 teaspoon ground turmeric
1 teaspoon salt
1/2 teaspoon white pepper
2 tablespoons freshly squeezed lemon juice
1 cup water
2 pounds fresh celery cut to 2" long, soaked in water
1/2 cup fresh Italian parsley

Heat oil in a pot and add garlic, cook 2 minutes on low heat while mixing constantly, add fresh ginger and turmeric, cook another minute, add water, lemon juice, white pepper, salt, and bring to a boil. Transfer celery sticks to the pot and bring to a boil, lower the heat, cover the pot, and cook for 30 minutes or until celery sticks are soft, add parsley in the last 5 minutes. To thicken the sauce—uncover the pot and simmer for about 5-7 minutes, check consistency, let cool down, refrigerate. Serve chilled.

YAFFA'S "NEVER LOOK AGAIN" FOR A POTATO SALAD 🍎— VEGETARIAN

1 pound potatoes peeled but leave whole
2 tablespoons fresh dill
2 green onions, chopped small
1/2 preserved lemons, chopped small
1/2 teaspoon white pepper
2 tablespoons capers
Optional—1/2 cup green pickled olives, no pits
1/4 cup olive oil
1/2 teaspoon white pepper
1/2 cup fresh Italian parsley
salt—the preserved lemon & capers are very salty, add salt only after tasting the ready salad

Bring a pot of water to a boil, add potatoes (no need to cube them yet), cook for 20 minutes to get soft potatoes but not too soft, transfer potatoes to a colander and drain all water. In a large mixing bowl add all other ingredients except salt and mix well, when the potatoes cool a little, cube potatoes and add to the marinade, gently fold in potatoes to preserve their cubed shape, taste to check if the salad needs salt, remember that the preserved lemons and the capers are salty enough and you might want to skip the salt step, store in refrigerator, serve chilled.

YAFFA'S ONE & ONLY — MATBUCHA, TOMATOES SALAD

4 pounds fresh soft tomatoes, cubed
1-pound green bell pepper
4 green hot peppers
7-10 large garlic cloves thinly sliced

1/2 teaspoon each salt and black pepper
1/4 cup olive oil

In a large pot place oil and garlic, cook for 3-4 minutes while mixing constantly, then add cubed tomatoes and mix well. Bring to a boil, reduce to low and cook covered for 1.5 hours. While the tomatoes are being cooked, broil the peppers to get dark spots on both sides, for a rustic smoky flavor do not peel off peppers skin. If you peel off the skin do not rinse peppers to keep some of that smoky old flavor. Slice both sweet and hot peppers to get long strips and set aside, after the tomatoes cook for 1.5 hours add peppers to tomatoes and mix well, add pepper and salt. and cook uncovered for another 1.5 hours on low heat while mixing every 15 minutes. Let the salad cool and refrigerate, serve chilled.

YAFFA'S ONE MORE "FALL IN LOVE" EGGPLANT OR ZUCCHINI — MOROCCO

4 eggplants washed skin on
1/2 cup olive oil
1/2 teaspoon black pepper
3 garlic cloves, minced
1/2-3/4 cup white vinegar
1 whole bunch of fresh cilantros, chopped small
2 tablespoons ground cumin

This is a large amount of marinade; you can cut all ingredients in half for a smaller amount. Preheat oven to 450F (230C). Make the marinade first, add vinegar, olive oil, cumin, cilantro, and minced garlic to a mixing bowl, mix to blend and set aside. Slice eggplants to a 1/2" thick, place eggplants on a foil-lined baking pan, brush eggplants with little olive oil, and brush both sides. Transfer eggplants to the oven and bake for 20-25 minutes until you can see that eggplants are soft, and some brown spots appear on them, take eggplants out of the oven and let cool for 10 minutes. Transfer eggplants to a large plate or a tray where they will be served, and set them up in a large circle, drizzle eggplants with this delicious marinade, make sure that each eggplant slice gets some of the marinade, cover with clear plastic wrap, and refrigerate until ready to serve. Serve chilled.

YAFFA'S ROASTED PEPPERS SALAD 🍎—VEGETARIAN

2.2 pounds bell peppers or hot jalapeños
1/2 teaspoon white pepper
1/4 cup olive oil
4-5 garlic cloves, minced
1/2 cup freshly squeezed lemon juice
1/2-1 teaspoon salt

Preheat the oven to broil, prepare marinade by adding lemon juice, salt, garlic, olive oil, and white pepper to a bowl, mix well and let sit for 15 minutes. Line a baking pan with foil and add peppers, broil 6-7 minutes on each side, make sure that the peppers have some burned dark spots but do not let them get burned completely, take peppers out of the oven and let them cool down. If you would like a more rustic smoky flavor do not peel off the peppers' skin, if you would like gentler flavor then to peel off the skin before mixing with the marinade. Clean peppers of all seeds and stems slice lengthwise, add peppers to the marinade and fold in gently to mix with marinade. Refrigerate, serve chilled.

YAFFA'S SURPRISING AVOCADO SURPRISE SALAD

3 fresh ripe avocados
2-3 tablespoons olive oil
2 tablespoons preserved lemons, chopped
2 tablespoons chives, thinly chopped
1/4 cup lemon juice
1/2 teaspoon each salt and pepper
1/2 teaspoon salt (do not add before final tasting)
1 tablespoon fresh Italian parsley, chopped

Make the marinade first, add all ingredients except the avocados to a mixing bowl, mix to blend, set aside, slice the avocados to halves and scoop out the inside, transfer to a small bowl, use a fork to mash avocados, transfer avocados to the marinade and fold in to blend, remember that the preserved lemons are salty so you might not need to add salt. Taste to check if more salt is needed. Refrigerate until serving, serve chilled.

Vegetables & Side Dishes

HELPFUL HINTS

- When preparing a casserole, make an additional batch to freeze for when you're short on time. Use within 2 months.
- To keep hot oil from splattering, sprinkle a little salt or flour in the pan before frying.
- To prevent pasta from boiling over, place a wooden spoon or fork across the top of the pot while the pasta is boiling.
- Boil all vegetables that grow above ground without a cover.
- Never soak vegetables after slicing; they will lose much of their nutritional value.
- Green pepper may change the flavor of frozen casseroles/ Clove, garlic, and pepper flavors get stronger when frozen, while sage, onion, and salt become milder.
- For an easy no-mess dish, grill vegetables along with your meat.
- Store dried pasta, rice (except brown rice), and whole grains in tightly covered containers in a cool, dry place. Refrigerate brown rice and freeze grains if you will not use them within 5 months.

- A few drops of lemon juice added to simmering rice will keep grains separated.
- When cooking greens, add a teaspoon of sugar to the water to help vegetables retain their fresh colors.
- To dress up buttered, cooked vegetables, sprinkle them with toasted sesame seeds, toasted chopped nuts, canned French-fried onions, grated cheese, or slightly crushed seasoned croutons.
- Soufflé dishes are designed with straight sides to help your soufflé rise. Ramekins work well for single-serve casseroles.
- A little vinegar or lemon juice added to potatoes before draining will make them extra white when mashed.
- To avoid toughened beans or corn, add salt midway through cooking.
- If your pasta sauce seems a little dry, add a few tablespoons of the pasta's cooking water.
- To prevent cheese from sticking to a grater, spray the grater with cooking spray before beginning.

BAKE OR FRY FETA & LEEK LATKES 🍎—VEGETARIAN

2 leeks, white parts only, chopped

2 potatoes, cooked and mashed

2 eggs

1 large garlic clove, minced

1/2 cup Italian parsley, chopped

1/4 cup fresh basil, chopped

2 tablespoon fresh dill, chopped

5 tablespoons mixed olive oil and vegetable oil

1/2 cup breadcrumbs

2/3 cup feta cheese

1/4-1/2 teaspoon black pepper

In a food processor add eggs, garlic, herbs, and potatoes. Pulse to mix 4-5 times. Add feta cheese, leeks, breadcrumbs, and black pepper, pulse twice. Do not add salt, the feta cheese is salty. Transfer to a bowl. Place oil in the pan, drizzle some oil on your hand to avoid sticking mixture, measure 1/4 cup of the filling and place in the pan, cook on medium heat, do not move the latke until it's time to flip it to the other side. Flip to the other side when the latke gets golden brown. Repeat with all latkes, transfer to a paper towel or colander to drain excess oil. This recipe yields about 8-10 latkes.

CELEBRATION OF SWEET & SAVORY RICE/NOODLES — IRAQ

2 tablespoon vegetables oil
1 medium onion, chopped
1 cup long grain rice
1/2 cup noodles, cooked or fried to add crispiness
1 teaspoon onion soup powder
3 tablespoon tomato paste
1/4 teaspoon salt and pepper
1/2 cup raisins
1 1/2 cups water

Place onion in a small pot, add oil, cook 5 minutes. Add 1 Cup long grain rice, Mix and cook 3-4 minutes. Add the water, mix and add tomato paste, mix to blend, add onion soup powder, mix, salt and pepper, noodles, raisins, mix well. Bring to a boil, reduce to simmer, cover and cook for about 20 minutes. The bottom of the pot will get caramelized, O yummy! Serve warm as a side dish, this recipe yields about 4 servings.

CHICKPEAS IN A COLORFUL SAUCE TO COMPLEMENT YOUR DINNER — ALGERIA ⭐—SPECIALTY

2-3 tablespoons olive oil

3 large garlic cloves, crushed

1-2 cayenne pepper (optional)

1 teaspoon cumin

1 teaspoon sweet paprika

1/2 teaspoon cinnamon

1 cup tomato sauce

1 cup water

1/2-1 teaspoon salt

4 cups dry chickpeas, soaked in water overnight

Place olive oil in a pot, add garlic cloves, cook 2 minutes on low heat to release aroma. If using cayenne pepper add it now. Add cumin, sweet paprika, gently shake the pot to blend flavors, add cinnamon, 1 cup tomato sauce, mix, cook 5 minutes while mixing. Add 1 cup of water, salt, chickpeas, gently mix to blend, cover, cook for one hour on low heat. Serve warm, this recipe yields 6-8 servings.

COLORFUL & AROMATIC, RICE & VEGETABLES DISH — BUCHARAH

3 cups basmati rice

3 tablespoons vegetable oil

2 onions sliced

2 teaspoon cumin seeds (not ground)

4 large carrots shredded

1 teaspoon each salt and black pepper

2/3 cup raisins

1 1/2 cups chickpeas, cooked
5 cups hot water

Soak the rice in water for one hour, drain, add salt and pepper, and set aside. Add oil to a pot, cook the onions and cumin seeds, add carrots, raisins, chickpeas, and mix, cook 5 minutes to blend flavors. Pour the rice on all the ingredients but do not mix, add water all the way 1/2" above the rice, bring to a boil, reduce the heat and cook to simmer until rice is soft and has absorbed all the liquids. Remove from heat and let rest covered for 10 minutes before serving. To serve, place rice on a plate and top with vegetables from the bottom of the pot. During the holidays it is customary to decorate with pomegranate seeds. This recipe yields up to 12 servings.

EASY TASTY PASTA DISH TO GO WITH EVERY MEAL — ISREAL ⏰—QUICK & EASY

1 pound pasta of any kind
1 large onion, chopped small
2 tablespoons each vegetable oil and olive oil
1 teaspoon salt
1 teaspoon sweet paprika
1/2 teaspoon turmeric

Cook pasta according to the instructions on the package, drain the water, and set aside. Place both oils in a pot, add onions, mix for 3-5 minutes. Add salt, turmeric, paprika, cook on low for 5 minutes, mix to blend flavors. Add the cooked pasta without water. Gently mix to blend and let the pasta absorb all the flavors. Optional—Add green peas or dill to flavor. Serve this pasta with every meal, this is a delicious comforting dish. This recipe yields about 5-6 servings as a side dish.

FETTUCCINE ALFREDO WITH A TWIST ITALY 🍎—VEGETARIAN

1 pound fettuccine pasta

1 tablespoon vegetable oil

2 1/2 cups heavy cream or plant based heavy cream

4 ounces salted butter or plant based butter

3 cups pecorino cheese

3 celery sticks

1/2 teaspoon each salt and pepper
1 cup green peas
1/2 cup fresh Italian parsley, chopped
1/4 cup fresh dill, chopped

Add 1 tablespoon vegetable oil to a pot filled with water, add pasta and celery to the pot, cook according to package instructions. Drain pasta and celery. Add butter to a pan, melt on low heat, add heavy cream, mix while adding. Gradually add pecorino to the pan while mixing to melt the cheese. Add salt and pepper, mix constantly. Add pasta and celery to the pan, add green peas, Cook and mix gently for another 5-7 minutes on low heat. Serve warmly. This recipe yields about 6-8 servings.

FOREVER POPULAR — SPAGHETTI, CHERRY TOMATO, IN GARLIC SAUCE — ITALY 🍎 —VEGETARIAN

1 pound spaghetti pasta
2/3 cup olive oil
12 garlic cloves, sliced
1 cup fresh cherry tomatoes, sliced
1/2 cup fresh Italian parsley, chopped
1/2 teaspoon each salt and pepper
1/2 cup pasta water (from the cooked pasta)
1/2 cup each pecorino Romano and Parmesan cheese

Cook the spaghetti pasta according to the package instructions, drain but reserve 1/2 cup of the water, set aside. Place garlic in the pan with olive oil, cook on medium for 1 minute to release aroma. Add the cherry tomatoes, mix in salt and pepper, add the spaghetti and gently mix to blend with the flavors. Add the pecorino Romano and mix. Add the parsley, parmesan, and the 1/2 cup cooked water. Gently mix to blend flavors, cook on low 5 more minutes uncovered. Serve warmly. This recipe yields 6-8 servings.

MAJADARA RICE & LENTILS PILAF — SYRIA ⏰—QUICK & EASY

1 cup lentils of any kind
6 tablespoon extra-virgin olive oil
2 large onions chopped
1/4 teaspoon cinnamon
1 cup basmati rice
1/4 cup fresh Italian parsley
1/2-1 teaspoon salt
1/4 teaspoon pepper

In a small saucepan combine water and salt & lentils, bring to a boil, reduce and cover, simmer for 30 minutes. Place oil in a large pan, sauté the onions until golden brown, add salt and pepper, and cinnamon, transfer to a colander, drain. In a separate pot cook the rice for about 15-20 minutes, add lentils to rice, mix to combine. Add onions and toss again to blend. Serve warm with some Parsley on top. This recipe yields about 5-7 servings.

QUICK PANTRY DELIGHT — LENTILS, RICE & CURRY ⭐— SPECIALTY

1 onion, chopped small
3 garlic cloves, minced
1 teaspoon fresh ginger, minced
1 tablespoon red curry paste
2 teaspoons red curry powder

1 cup red lentils

1 teaspoon salt

1 cup coconut milk

1 cup diced tomatoes

2 cups basmati rice or quinoa

1 cup garbanzo beans (optional)

2 tablespoons fresh cilantro for decoration

juice of one lemon

1 tablespoon coconut oil

Fill up a pot with water, cook the rice with salt for 10 minutes. Pour the rice into a colander, run cold water to rinse the rice and stop the cooking process. Add the coconut oil, onions, minced garlic, and ginger to a pan, mix to blend. Add both curries, mix, add coconut milk, simmer for 3 minutes, add tomatoes, mix, add lentils, mix, add cooked rice, lemon juice, and garbanzo beans if using, mix to blend. Cover and simmer for 10 minutes. Let sit covered for 5 minutes before serving. Decorate with fresh cilantro leaves. Serve warm, this recipe yields about 4-5 servings.

RICE WITH ANGEL HAIR — ISRAEL, LEBANON, TURKEY, EGYPT 🍎—VEGETARIAN

2 cup basmati rice

1/4 cup vegetable oil

2 cups vermicelli pasta

3 cups hot water

1 teaspoon salt

1 teaspoon Baharat spice mix (see recipe in This and That category)

Heat oil in a pot, add the vermicelli pasta, fry to golden brown. Add rice and cook with pasta for 5 more minutes. Add water, Baharat, and salt, cover and cook for 20 minutes. Remove from the heat, let the rice rest covered in the pot for another 10 minutes. Fluff the rice with a fork before serving. Serve warm, this recipe yields about 6-8 servings.

TASTY BEANS TO COMPLEMENT EVERY MEAL — TUNISIA 🍎— VEGETARIAN

1 cup black beans
1/2 cup olive oil
4 garlic cloves, minced
1 teaspoon sweet or hot paprika
2 tablespoons tomato paste or diced tomatoes
1/3 cup freshly squeezed lemon juice
1 1/2 teaspoons caraway
1 tablespoon cumin
1/2 teaspoon salt

Place black beans in a small pot, add lemon juice, mix to blend. Add all other ingredients, mix to blend. Bring to a boil, cover, reduce, and simmer 30-40 minutes. This is a tasty dish served with plain rice or pasta. Serve warm or cold. When I have a busy day, and there is no time to cook, I make this dish and serve it with tortilla chips and a freshly cut salad. This recipe yields about 3-4 servings.

TASTY CABBAGE SIDE DISH TO COMPLEMENT EVERY MEAL — ISRAEL

2-3 tablespoons vegetable oil (no olive oil)
5 garlic cloves, sliced
1 onion, chopped
1 teaspoon turmeric

1 teaspoon sweet paprika

1 cup water

1/4 teaspoon black pepper

1/2-1 teaspoon salt

1 teaspoon onion soup powder

1 large tomato, grated

1 large green cabbage, sliced, washed (no purple cabbage)

1/2 teaspoon chili flax (optional)

juice of 1 lemon

Place oil in a pot, add onions and garlic, cook for 3 minutes on medium heat. In a separate bowl add grated tomato, turmeric, paprika, salt, black pepper, mix to blend. Add 1/2 of the tomato mixture to the onions. Cook for 3 minutes, start adding the cabbage, if the pot is filled but you have extra cabbage, cover, cook for a few minutes, it will start being soft enough to make room for the rest of the cabbage. Gently mix to blend the flavors. Cook for about 30-40 minutes, add the lemon juice and gently mix to blend. Serve warm with any main dish, this recipe yields up to 8 servings.

THE FAMOUS MAGADARAH, SAVORY RICE & LENTIL — SYRIA 🍎—VEGETARIAN

2 cups long grain rice

1 cup brown lentils

4 tablespoons olive oil

3 onions chopped

1 teaspoon cumin

1 teaspoon salt

1/2 teaspoon black pepper

1 onion, sliced into circles

1 egg
1/2 cup flour

Start by cooking the brown lentils for 30 minutes in water, drain and set aside. Place oil in a pan, add chopped onions, cook to brown. Add lentils, salt, and pepper. Add the rice, mix for 2-3 minutes. Add 3 cups hot water, bring to a boil, reduce and simmer covered 20 minutes. Let the pot sit covered for 10 minutes after you turn off the heat. While the rice is resting make the crispy onion rings. Place some oil in a pan, dip the onion rings in an egg, then dip it in the flour, and fry for a few minutes on each side. To serve—Fluff the rice/lentils mixture with a fork, transfer one serving to a plate, decorate with 2-3 onion rings, serve warm. This recipe yields about 4-6 servings.

VENETIAN RISOTTO WITH PEAS & CELERY — ITALY

1/4 cup olive oil
4 shallots or green onions, chopped
4 celery sticks, chopped
1 1/2 cups Arborio rice
4 cups water
1 tablespoon chicken consume
4 tablespoons olive oil or butter
1/2 cup parmesan cheese
1/2 teaspoon each salt and pepper

Add olive oil to the pan, add celery, shallots, cook for 8 minutes. Add rice mix for 2 minutes. Add half of the water and chicken consume, cook 3 minutes. Add the other half of the water, bring it to a boil, reduce and cook to absorb all liquids. Add green peas, gently mix to blend. Cover again, cook for 5 more minutes on simmer. Add parmesan, salt, and pepper, and gently mix. This recipe yields up to 6 servings.

YAFFA'S AWARD-WINNING HOLIDAYS CENTERPIECE FLOWER — ROASTED VEGETABLES TERRINE ⭐—SPECIALTY

4 yellow bell peppers

4 red bell peppers

4 green bell peppers

4 eggplants with skin

2 yellow zucchinis

2 green zucchinis

5 tablespoons Agar Agar vegan gelatin or any other gelatin

4 cups diced tomatoes, or 4 cup tomato matbucha salad (see recipe in the Soup and Salads category)

10 garlic cloves, sliced

small bowl of olive oil for brushing olive oil

1 large bunch fresh basil leaves, leaves only

2 tablespoons homemade harissa, (optional for taste see recipe in This and That category)

1 teaspoon salt

1 cup water

1/2 teaspoon black pepper

1 package of clear plastic wrap

1 round bunt cake baking dish

Preheat oven to broil, slice all bell peppers to get 3 wide parts from each bell pepper, slice eggplants and zucchini as well, each slice should not be more than 1/4" thick, discard the stem, head, and all seeds from the peppers, brush with olive oil on both sides and place in a foil-lined baking tray. Bake until a few brown/dark roasted spots show on the bell pepper on each side, repeat with all peppers, eggplants, and zucchini slices, keep all vegetables in separate bowls, keep colors of peppers in separate bowls as well. While the vegetables are being roasted, place tomatoes in a food processor, mix to grind to make a sauce, add olive oil and garlic to a pan, add about 10 small basil leaves, cook on low heat to release aroma, about 3-4 minutes, pour tomato puree on the garlic and mix to blend, cook covered for 30 minutes on low heat, add 5 table-spoon Agar Agar gelatin to a small pot, add water, mix, boil for 1 minute, add the gelatin to the tomatoes, add Harissa paste, cook another 10 minutes, mix to blend. Line a bundt cake baking pan with clear plas-tic, the whole inside of the bundt pan should be covered with clear plastic plus extra on the outside to cover the top later. Start with the fresh basil leaves, choose the largest leaves, place one leaf inside the wall of the baking pan, repeat all around the inside walls of the baking dish. Next layer is the eggplants, generously dip one slice of eggplant in the tomato sauce, place the eggplant slice on the basil leaf, repeat with all the circle of basil leaves to cover with dipped slices of eggplants and tomato sauce, add another fresh basil leaf on each eggplant slice, dip a bell pepper generously in the tomato sauce and cover the second basil leaf, add the 3rd basil leaf all around the bell peppers and add a different color of bell pepper dipped generously in the tomato sauce. Each circle of vegetables should be dipped with a lot of tomato sauce, remember that the tomato sauce will be congealed with the gelatin to help form the beautiful shape of the flower terrine at the end. Repeat with all eggplants, zucchini, and bell peppers until the whole bundt cake baking pan is filled with layers of vegetables, basil leaves, and tomato sauce in between the layers. When all the pan is stuffed drizzle on top any extra tomato sauce and try to push it in between the layers, take the extra clear plastic that was reserved on the sides and cover the top of the pan to secure from leaking. Wrap the whole pan with clear plastic wrap at least twice to secure more and help the layers to stick together. Place heavy food cans all around the wrapped baking pan to create more weight, refrigerate overnight. When you are ready to serve, remove all the heavy weight, use scissors to cut the top clear plastic, place a large round plate on top of the terrine and flip to the other side, gently pull off the bundt baking dish, careful not to shake it too much to preserve the flower shape. Peel off all remaining plastic wrap, place it in the middle of the table as a centerpiece. Serve cold as a vegetable side dish, or a vegan main dish. Do not take it out of the fridge before you are ready to serve. This beautiful flower terrine will yield about 10-13 servings.

YAFFA'S REFRESHING SALAD, GREEN & YELLOW ZUCCHINI IN LEMON DILL SAUCE

2 zucchinis, sliced
2 tablespoons olive oil
1/2 teaspoon each salt and pepper
2 cups water

juice of 1 lemon
2 tablespoons fresh dill, chopped

In a pot place all ingredients except the zucchini and dill. Bring the sauce to a boil, add zucchini and gently mix to blend. Simmer covered for 10 minutes then uncover and cook for another few minutes to thicken the sauce. Transfer to a serving dish and sprinkle dill on top. Serve warm or cold. This dish is even better the next day. This recipe yields 4 servings.

YAFFA'S SAVORY — THE POPULAR YELLOW RICE WE SERVED IN MY RESTAURANT ⭐—SPECIALTY

2 cups basmati rice
2 tablespoons olive oil
1 teaspoon each salt, black pepper, turmeric
1 tablespoon each dry basil, dry marjoram, dry dill
4 cups water

This rice is so simple but was very loved in my restaurant, there was never a request for not including this rice in a dish. Also, it goes with a lot of different dishes, even though is flavored and not plain rice. Start by soaking the rice in cold water for 10 minutes, dump the cloudy water and refill with fresh water, repeat 3-4 times until the last water comes out clear and that is your sign that the rice does not have any more starch in it. Place the rice in a small pot, add olive oil, and cook for 2-3 minutes. Add all other ingredients and bring to a boil, reduce, cover, simmer for 20 minutes. This recipe yields 4-6 servings.

YAFFA'S TASTY QUINOA IN CARAMELIZED ONION 🍎 — VEGETARIAN

3 tablespoons vegetable oil
1 large onion, chopped small
2 cups water
2 cups quinoa
1 teaspoon salt
1/2 teaspoon each black pepper and turmeric

Place onions and oil in a small pot, cook to brown, approximately 5-7 minutes. Add all other ingredients, bring to a boil, reduce, cover, and cool for 20 minutes. Use a fork to fluff and air the quinoa. This recipe yields about 6 servings.

YAFFA'S THANKSGIVING GRAVY... SEPHARDIC STYLE ⭐ — SPECIALTY

2 cups of ice water

the oils and liquid that came out of the turkey
1/4 cup corn starch
1/4 cup flour
1/2-1 teaspoon salt

Scrape all the oils and liquid that came out from roasting the turkey, add 1/2-1 teaspoon salt, add flour, corn starch, and water, cook on medium to low while mixing constantly, let the gravy thicken to your liking; keep covered until served.

YAFFA'S THANKSGIVING STUFFING... SEPHARDIC STYLE ⭐— SPECIALTY

2 cups Israeli couscous
1 large onion, chopped
1 cup carrots, cubed
1 cup celery, cubed
1 cup sweet potato, cubed (optional)
1/2 teaspoon salt

Cook the chopped onions with oil, to brown, add turmeric, salt, mix &
cook for 2 more minutes, add all vegetables and water, bring to a boil,
reduce heat, cover, and simmer for 20-25 minutes.

HELPFUL HINTS

- Certain meats, like ribs and pot roast, can be parboiled before grilling to reduce the fat content.
- Pound meat lightly with a mallet or rolling pic, pierce with a fork, sprinkle lightly with meat tenderizer, and add marinade. Refrigerate for 20 minutes and cook or grill for a quick and succulent meat.
- Marinating is a cinch if you use a plastic bag. The meat stays in the marinade and it's easy to turn. Cleanup is easy; just toss the bag.
- It's easier to thinly slice meat if it's partially frozen.
- Adding tomatoes to roasts naturally tenderizes the meat as tomatoes contain an acid that works well to break down meats.
- Whenever possible, cut meat across the grain; this will make it easier to eat and also give it a more attractive appearance.
- When frying meat, sprinkle paprika on the meat to turn it golden brown.
- Thaw all meats in the refrigerator for maximum safety.

- Refrigerate poultry promptly after purchasing. Keep it in the coldest part of your refrigerator for up to 2 days. Freeze poultry for longer storage. Never leave poultry at room temperature for over 2 hours.
- When frying chicken, canola oil provides a milder taste, and it contains healthier amounts of saturated and polyunsaturated fats. Do not cover the chicken once it has finished cooking because covering will cause the coating to lose its crispness.
- One pound of boneless chicken equals approximately 3 cups of cubed chicken.
- Generally, red meats should reach 160° and poultry should reach 180° before serving. If preparing fish, the surface of the fish should flake off with a fork.
- Rub lemon juice on fish before cooking to enhance the flavor and help maintain a good color.
- Scaling a fish is easier if vinegar is rubbed on the scales first.
- When grilling fish, the rule of thumb is to cook 5 minutes on each side per inch of thickness. For example, cook a 2-inch-thick fillet for 10 minutes per side. Before grilling, rub with oil to seal in moisture.

BERKOK, THE DAIRY PURIM COUSCOUS — MOROCCO 🌺 —IN MEMORY

1 pound durum semolina
3-4 cups water
4 1/2 cups milk
1 teaspoon cinnamon
1/2 cup sugar
4 ounces unsalted butter, cubed

This dairy couscous was served as a meal after the fast on Purim, it resembles breakfast grits and reminds me how fascinating it is to know all the similarities in dishes from all over the world. Make the couscous first—Place the semolina in a pot and add the water, bring to a boil, reduce, cover, and simmer for 20-30 minutes until semolina absorbs all the water. Add the cinnamon and sugar, cook on low until the mixture thickens, mix the whole time, otherwise the bottom of the pot will burn the semolina. Serve in small bowls and add one cube of butter to each serving. This recipe yields 6-7 servings.

BEST EVER, SO EASY, CHICKEN GYROS — GREECE ⏰—QUICK & EASY

1/2 cup olive oil
2 tablespoons fresh oregano leaves
1 teaspoon lemon zest
1/2 teaspoon black pepper
1 teaspoon coriander
1/2 teaspoon salt
1/2 teaspoon chili flex (optional)

1 teaspoon sweet paprika
1 tablespoon fresh thyme
2 pounds chicken pieces, preferably thighs
oregano tahini (see recipe in This and That category)

In a mixing bowl add all ingredients except the chicken and the oregano Tahini. Brush each piece of chicken with the marinade. Refrigerate for one hour, but preferably overnight. Add 2 tablespoon olive oil to a pan, add chicken pieces, add all marinade juices, sear chicken on high heat for 5 minutes only, while mixing constantly. The chicken will cook a few more minutes after you remove it from the heat. Serve on a toasted pita bread, drizzle on the oregano Tahini (see recipe in This and That category) serve warm.

CHORSHET SABZI — PERSIAN DELIGHT — IRAN ⭐—SPECIALTY

2.2 pounds beef (shoulder cut), cubed medium
1/2 cup vegetable oil
3 onions, chopped
2/3 cup red beans, soaked in water overnight
3 dried lemons (black dry lemons can be found in Middle East stores)
1/2 teaspoon salt
1 teaspoon each black pepper and turmeric
5 cup boiling water
2 bunches of fresh parsley, leaves only, chopped small
1 bunch for dill, leaves only, chopped
1 bunch of celery leaves, chopped
1 bunch of cilantros, leaves and stems, chopped small
1 bunch of green onion, chopped small
1 leek, white part only, chopped small
1/2 cup lemon juice

In a pot place 1/4 cup oil and onion, cook 8 minutes, add meat cubes and cook to brown. Add red beans, dried lemons, salt, pepper, turmeric, and water, bring to a boil, reduce and simmer covered for one hour. Place the rest of the oil in a pan, add all chopped herbs, green onion, and leek, cook for 8-10 minutes to become translucent, add salt, transfer to the pot with the meat and gently mix in. Cover partially the pot, cook on simmer for another 1 1/2 hours until the meat is soft. Add lemon juice and cook another 5-7 minutes, taste to see if more salt is needed. Serve warm with plain rice. This dish yields about 7-8 servings.

CHRAYME, THE FLAG SHABBAT FISH DISH — TUNISIA & LIBYA ⭐—SPECIALTY

1/4 cup vegetable oil
1 teaspoon sugar
1 teaspoon caraway seeds
1/2 cup tomato paste
1 tablespoon sweet paprika
1/2-1 teaspoon cayenne pepper (optional)
1 teaspoon salt
8 garlic cloves, chopped
1 1/2 tablespoons Harissa (see recipe in This and That category)
1 teaspoon fresh lemon zest
1 bunch each cilantro and dill
2 pounds salmon, sliced to 2" x 3" per a serving
3 cup water

Place herbs and garlic in a large pan, add tomato paste, paprika, cayenne if using, caraway, lemon zest, salt, Harissa (see recipe in This and that category), sugar and water, mix, bring to a boil, reduce and cover, simmer 50 minutes. Transfer the salmon slices to the sauce, cover all the fish with sauce. Bring the fish to a boil, reduce and cover. Simmer salmon for 15 minutes. Serve warm with plenty of crispy bread to enjoy this delicious sauce. This recipe yields about 10 servings.

CLASSIC & SOOO TASTY SHABBAT FISH DISH — MOROCCO ⭐— SPECIALTY

6 large pieces of white fish- sea bass, cod, mahi mahi
1/2 cup olive oil

3 dry long chili pepper such as ancho, California
2 cups water
2 red hot peppers or red bell peppers
8-10 garlic cloves
2 tablespoons sweet red paprika
1 cup fresh cilantro, chopped
1 cup fresh parsley, chopped

Place oil in a wide pan, add both red peppers and garlic and cook for 3 minutes. Add paprika, salt and pepper, cook another 3 minutes. Add water and bring to a boil. Add the fish, cover and simmer for about 20 minutes. To thicken the sauce, remove the lid and simmer another 10 minutes or until the sauce is thickened to desire consistency. Serve warm, accompanied by a slice of lemon.

COLD SERVED SALMON WITH SALSA VERDE — ITALY ⭐ — SPECIALTY

For the fish—
6-7 pounds salmon or Mahi Mahi
1/2 cup olive oil
1/4 teaspoon each salt and pepper
Juice of half lemon

For the Salsa Verde—
1/2 bunch fresh Italian parsley, chopped
2.5 oz. pine nuts
5 small pickles
3 garlic cloves, minced
8 green olives, pitted
lemon juice from one lemon

salt and pepper
1 cup cold press olive oil

Preheat the oven to 400F (200C). Start by brushing the fish with olive oil, add salt and pepper, wrap with foil and transfer to the oven. Bake for 40 minutes, remove from oven, but reserve all liquids from baking. Let the fish cool down in the wrapped foil. Add the liquids from the baking to a small bowl, mix with olive oil and lemon juice, drizzle on the fish. Cover the fish again and refrigerate for overnight. Make the salsa Verde—place all ingredients except the olive oil in a food processor, pulse 34 times only, to get a chopped mixture, do not grind. Gradually add the olive oil to the food processor to blend. Taste to see if more salt and pepper are needed. Serve this fish cold from the refrigerator, top with salsa Verde and add crispy bread for dipping. Optional—some Italians like to add other herbs such as dill, basil, or chives, but it is not part of the classic recipe. This recipe yields 8 -10 servings.

DELIGHTFUL FISH COUSCOUS FOR EVERY OCCASION — TUNISIA ⭐—SPECIALTY

2-3 pounds fish of any kind, preferably white, sliced to large pieces

1/4 cup olive oil

2 onions chopped

2 celery sticks

6 garlic cloves minced

4 tomatoes, diced

1/4-1/2 teaspoon cayenne pepper (optional)

1 teaspoon sweet paprika

1 tablespoon ground cumin

1/2 teaspoon black pepper

6 cups water or chicken stock

1 cup cooked chickpeas

3 carrots, peeled, cut to large pieces

5-7 small potatoes

Juice of half lemon (optional)

4 tablespoon fresh mint, chopped
1-2 tablespoons Harissa

In a large pot add onions, celery, garlic, and cook for 10 minutes on low heat. Add diced tomatoes, Harissa, cayenne if using, sweet paprika, and black pepper. Cook for a few minutes. Add water, chickpeas, carrots, and simmer for 20 minutes. Add fish and potatoes and simmer to soften the potatoes and the fish, about 20 minutes. Add lemon juice and mint if using. To serve, place some couscous on a plate, top with fish and some of the vegetables and ladle broth to cover. This recipe yields about 8-10 servings.

EASY & DELICIOUS CHICKEN MARSALA — ITALY ⭐ — SPECIALTY

5 pieces of chicken breast sliced to 1/4" thick
1 cup flour or gluten-free flour
4 tablespoons olive oil
10 oz. cremini mushrooms, sliced
1 cup chicken stock
4 garlic cloves chopped small
3 shallots sliced small
1/2 teaspoon each salt and pepper
1 cup Marsala wine
2 more tablespoons olive oil
1/4 cup fresh Italian parsley, chopped

Place flour in a bowl next to the chicken breast, set aside. In a pan add olive oil, dip chicken breast in the flour and coat all over. Transfer to the pan and cook to brown both sides, about 4 minutes, transfer to a bowl to drain excess oil. Add garlic and shallots to the same pan, cook for 2-3 minutes. Add sliced mushrooms, mix, cook for 5 minutes. Add salt, pepper, mix for a minute. Add Marsala wine, chicken stock, mix, bring to a boil, reduce heat, and cook to about a half of the size of the sauce for about 30 minutes, the sauce should get thicker which is our goal. Now you can return the chicken breast back to the pan, sprinkle the fresh parsley. Continue to cook for 3 more minutes and you are going to enjoy a restaurant dish in the comfort of your home, cheers. Serve warm on a plate with the mushrooms and drizzles the sauce on top. This recipe yields about 4-5 servings.

ESPECIALLY FOR PAELLA LOVERS — SPAIN, PORTUGAL, MOROCCO ⭐—SPECIALTY

2 tablespoons olive oil

4 pounds chicken thighs

1 1/2 teaspoons salt

1 cup water

2 onions, chopped

2 large garlic cloves, chopped

1 large tomato

2 bay leaves

1 teaspoon sweet paprika

5 saffron threads

3 zucchinis, cut large

4 carrots, cut large

2 green squashes, cut large

1 1/2 cups water

1/2 teaspoon thyme

1/2-1 teaspoon dry oregano or sage

1/2 teaspoon black pepper

1 1/2 cups arborio rice or basmati

1/2 teaspoon turmeric

1 1/2 cups water for the rice

In a wide pan add oil and chicken, brown the chicken pieces to golden brown, transfer chicken pieces to a different pot. Do not discard the oil. Add water and salt to the new chicken pot, bring to a boil, reduce heat and simmer for 30 minutes. In the same pan with the same oil add onions and brown, add garlic, cook 4-5 minutes. Shred the tomato right on the pan with onions and garlic. Cook tomato onion mixture for 5 minutes on low heat. While the tomato is cooking add bay leaves, black pepper, turmeric, sweet paprika, and saffron threads, mix. Add vegetables, water and bring to a boil, cover, reduce heat, simmer for 15 minutes. Add dry oregano, thyme, and cover, cook for 5 minutes. Add back chicken pieces to the wide pan, add rice in between all the chicken pieces and vegetables. Push the rice to the bottom of the pot to soak in some of the flavors. Drizzle all the liquid from the cooked chicken on the rice, add 1 1/2 cups water, tilt a little to blend flavors, cover, simmer for 40 minutes. Serve warmly with fresh salad. This recipe yields 6 servings.

FISH WITH SAFFRON SAUCE — MOROCCO ⭐—SPECIALTY

4 tablespoons olive oil

4-5 garlic cloves, chopped

2 teaspoons turmeric

1/2 teaspoon salt

1/4 teaspoon white pepper

1/2 teaspoon saffron threads, steeped in 5 tablespoons hot water for 5 minutes

2 lemons, peeled, seeds removed and cubed

1 bunch of fresh cilantros, chopped

4-6 fish fillet such as sea bass, halibut, mahi mahi, cod, salmon

In a small bowl place lemon, turmeric, salt, and pepper. Press the lemon cubes to release lemon juice. Add 1 tablespoon olive oil, set aside. Place the garlic in a large pan, sauté on very low heat with olive oil for 3 minutes, add the saffron with the water. Add cubed lemons without the lemon juice to the pan and some of the chopped cilantro, place the fish fillet on top and add the reserved lemon juice on the fish fillet. Sprinkle with the rest of the fresh cilantro. Bring to a boil, reduce the heat, cover, and simmer for only 8-10 minutes. Some communities sprinkle cumin at the end of the cooking, it is optional. This recipe yields about 6 servings.

HOUSEWARMING & HOLIDAYS COUSCOUS — MOROCCO

2 large onions chopped

2 soft tomatoes, shredded

2 1/2 pounds meat of your choice such as chicken, beef, lamb

1/2 teaspoon sweet paprika

1/2 teaspoon turmeric

1/4 teaspoon saffron threads steeped in 1/4 cup hot water

1 teaspoon fresh ginger minced

1/2 teaspoon cinnamon

1 tablespoon chicken powder

1/2 teaspoon white pepper

1/2 cup raisins

1 cup dates, pitted

1 cup dry prunes, pitted

1/2 cup almonds, peeled

5 large carrots, cut to quarters

2-3 large, sweet potatoes, cut to quarters

1 pound pumpkin

2 tablespoons brown sugar

2 tablespoons honey

2 cups durum semolina

Place onions in a large pot, cook on medium until golden brown, add shredded tomato and keep mixing while cooking for 5-7 minutes. Add spices, sugar, and honey cook for one minute to blend. Add the meat of your choice, cover and simmer another 7-8 minutes for the meat to release flavor. Add only 2 cups of water, bring to a boil, cover, reduce, and simmer for 20 minutes. Fill up the pot with water, about a half of the height of the pot, add chickpeas, vegetables, bring to a boil, reduce, cover, and cook for 30 minutes. Taste and add salt if needed, cover and cook for one hour. Make the semolina couscous—Add semolina to a pot, add 4 cups water, bring to a boil, reduce to simmer, cover, and simmer for 20-25 minutes. Keep pot covered to let the steam work after cooking as well. Place steamed semolina on a serving plate, top with some couscous soup, meat, and vegetables. Serve warm, this recipe yields about 8 servings.

KARP FISH BALLS IN CHRAYME SAUCE — LIBYA ⭐ — SPECIALTY

For the fish balls—
1 pound Karp fish
2 eggs
1/4 cup breadcrumbs
1/2 teaspoon each salt and pepper
1/2 teaspoon each nutmeg, coriander
1/2 cup fresh cilantro, chopped

For the chrayme sauce—
3 tablespoons olive oil
4 large garlic cloves, minced

1 tablespoon sweet paprika

1 teaspoon hot paprika

7 ounces tomato paste

1 teaspoon ground caraway seeds

salt—taste before adding

Mix all ingredients for fish balls and refrigerate for 30 minutes. In a wide pan place oil and garlic, simmer for 3 minutes on low heat, add both red paprikas, mix and cook for a minute, add tomato sauce, caraway, and salt if adding, cook for 2 minutes, add one cup water, bring to a boil, reduce heat, and simmer while adding the fish balls, cook for 15 more minutes. Serve warm on a bed of plain rice or plain couscous. This recipe yields 5-6 servings.

KEBAB FROM THE FAMOUS "AL BABOOR RESTAURANT" STYLE ☆—SPECIALTY

2.2 pounds ground lamb

1 teaspoon salt

1/2 teaspoon Baharat spice mix (see recipe in This and That category)

4 tomatoes

1 large garlic clove, minced

1 green pepper, spicy

2 onions, cut to quarters

Pita dough for the kebab baking (see recipe in Breads category)

"Al Baboor" kebabs are known for their unique flavors, they are grilled on hot charcoals and only then transferred to an oven. If you follow this recipe exactly you are going to be rewarded with a unique celebrated flavor of kebabs. If you don't have charcoals, start grilling in a broiling oven then switch to a baking oven, this will be the closest method to the real thing. Preheat oven to 400F (200C). Mix the ground meat with the salt and Baharat, shaped like long oval meatballs. Grill the tomatoes and peel off the skin. Cube the tomatoes, add garlic, hot green pepper, mix. Add one oval meat ball to a skewer, now add quarter onion, add another meat ball and another quarter onion. Grill for 3 minutes on each side. Remove from the grill and transfer to a baking dish. Add grilled tomatoes to the baking pan, cover each kebab with one circle of dough, bake for 10 minutes. Transfer one kebab with one baked pita to a plate, add some of the tomato garlic on it. Fold in one kebab and enjoy. This recipe yields up to 6 servings.

KEBABS WRAPPED AROUND CINNAMON STICKS ⏰—QUICK & EASY

1.5 pounds ground beef or chicken
2 teaspoons Lekama spice mix (see recipe in This and That category)
2 tablespoons fresh parsley, leaves only, chopped
1 tablespoon fresh cilantro, chopped
4 large garlic cloves, minced
2/3-1 teaspoon salt
10-16 cinnamon sticks

I first saw this great idea in a cookbook from Karen Nachimovski and loved the idea, so I decided to apply it a little differently and added it to my recipe for kebabs, the results came out great and delicious. Preheat oven to 425F (218C). Place all ingredients except the cinnamon sticks in a bowl, mix well. Refrigerate for 30 minutes for the flavors to blend. Line a baking pan with foil and brush the baking pan with a little olive oil. Set a small bowl with olive oil next to you in the workspace. Each kebab should be about 1/3 cup of ground meat. Wrap the meatball around one cinnamon stick, the stick should be all covered with the ground meat, place on the baking pan, repeat with all other sticks and meat ball kebabs. Transfer to the oven, bake for 7-10 minutes, remember the kebabs are still cooking for another few minutes after they are out of the oven. Serve these kebabs on a bed of greens, pasta, quinoa, or rice. This recipe yields about 8-10 servings.

LEMON CHICKEN PORTUGUESE DELIGHT — PORTUGAL

2 tablespoons ground cumin
2 teaspoons sweet paprika
3/4 teaspoon salt
1/4 teaspoon black pepper
5 tablespoons fresh cilantro, chopped
Juice of 2 freshly squeezed lemons
1/4 cup olive oil
2 pounds of chicken thighs or legs
1 medium onion
1 1/2 tablespoons garlic, minced
1 cup each—dry white wine, chicken broth
10 slices of fresh lemon

Place cumin, paprika, salt, black pepper, chopped cilantro, and lemon juice in a bowl, mix well. Rub this paste mixture on the chicken. Cover the bowl, marinade chicken for 2 hours or overnight. Place olive oil in a pan, sauté chicken pieces on both sides. Cover and cook for 5 minutes. Add onions, garlic, and add leftover chicken liquids if there are any, mix well, cook covered for 10 minutes. Add white wine, add chicken broth. Optional—add 2 tablespoons chopped cilantro. Cover, cook on low for 40 minutes. Add slices of lemons. Every once in while drizzle a little sauce on the lemon slices as well. Serve warm, this recipe yields 4-6 servings.

MAMA'S CHICKEN TAGINE WITH GREEN OLIVES & PRESERVED LEMON — MOROCCO 🌺—IN MEMORY

6 garlic cloves, sliced

1/4 cup olive oil

1/2 teaspoon turmeric

1/2 teaspoon white pepper

2 soft tomatoes, diced

8 chicken thighs

1/2 preserved lemon, sliced to 8 parts (see recipe in This and That category)

1/2 cup lemon juice

3 tablespoons fresh parsley, chopped

1 cup pickled green olives, pitted

2 cups water

1/4 teaspoon salt—taste before adding!

If you don't have a tagine, use a wide deep pan or wide pot. Place garlic and olive oil in a pan, cook on low for 2 minutes, add turmeric, pepper, and cook another 1-2 minutes, add diced tomatoes, add chicken thighs, brown for 2-3 minutes to release flavors and liquids. Add preserved lemons, lemon juice, olives, and sprinkle with parsley. Add water, bring to a boil, reduce the heat, and cover. Cook for 30 minutes, open the lid halfway, keep cooking on low heat for another 30 minutes; this will reduce the liquids and thicken the sauce. Please remember that the olives and preserved lemons are both salty, so you might not want to add salt, taste to check if more salt is needed. Serve warm with plain rice or pasta. If using a tagine reduce water amount to 1 cup. This recipe yields 8 servings.

MAMA'S HEARTWARMING COUSCOUS — MOROCCO

2 medium onions chopped

1/4 cup mixed vegetable oil and olive oil

3-5 garlic cloves, sliced

2 soft tomatoes, shredded

2 1/2 pounds meat of your choice such as chicken, beef, lamb

1 1/2 cups chickpeas, soaked in water overnight

1 teaspoon each salt, pepper, sweet paprika

1/2 teaspoon turmeric

1 tablespoon chicken powder

1/4 teaspoon saffron steeped in 2 tablespoons hot water

5 large carrots

1 pound pumpkin

5 zucchinis

3 large potatoes, cut to quarters

4 celery sticks

2 tablespoons Italian parsley

water for the soup

2 cups durum semolina

Place onions in a large pot, cook on medium until golden brown, add garlic and cook 1 more minute, reduce to simmer, add shredded tomato and keep mixing while cooking for 5-7 minutes. Add spices and cook for one minute to blend. Add the meat of your choice, cover and simmer another 7-8 minutes for the meat to release flavor. Add only 2 cups of water, bring to a boil, cover, reduce, and simmer for 20 minutes. Fill up the pot with water, about half of the height of the pot, add chickpeas, vegetables, and herbs, bring to a boil, reduce, cover, and cook for 30 minutes, taste and add salt if needed, cover and cook another 30 minutes. Make the semolina couscous—Add semolina to a pot, add 4 cups water, bring to a boil, reduce to simmer, cover, and simmer for 20-25 minutes. Keep pot covered to let the steam work after cooking. Place steamed semolina on a serving plate, top with some couscous soup, meat and vegetables. Serve warm, this recipe yields about 8 servings.

MAMA'S SAVORY CHAMIN, SCHINA, DEFINA, CHULENT & SHABBAT GOODNESS FOREVER — MOROCCO

For the Chamin—

8 chicken pieces legs and thighs

3 cups dry chickpeas

1-2 large, sweet potato do peel

2 large garlic heads, do not peel, keep the whole head together

2 large soup bones

1 pound beef for stew, cubed

1 teaspoon salt

1 teaspoon turmeric

1/4 cup vegetable oil

a few small round potatoes, do not peel skin

eggs, one for each guest

1 sweet log of meat and aromatic skin, spices (see separate recipe in Main Dishes category)

1 savory log of tasty wheat (see recipe inside Dishes category)

In a large enough pot that will accommodate all other chamin ingredients place all the chickpeas in the bottom of the pot. Slice the top of the 2 garlic heads, just enough to expose the garlic cloves, do not separate the garlic cloves, just rinse the back part that has some root hair to get rid of dust and dirt, place the 2 garlic heads in the large pot as well, you can add the little pieces of garlic that you took off to the wheat cookie bag later. Add chicken and beef and all other ingredients for the chamin, add the sweet and savory meat logs, add the tasty whole wheat cookie bag, cover, bring to a boil, reduce to medium and cook for 2 hours. Transfer to an oven and bake for a minimum of 8-12 hours. The chamin will spread a nice warm aroma in your kitchen, chamin is a great comforting food usually during the winter months. This recipe yields about 12 servings or even more. If making for a small number of guests divide ingredients into half. Serve warm, right from the oven for Shabbat lunch.

MAMA'S TAGINE CHICKEN OF THE SAHARA WILDERNESS — BERBERS OF MOROCCO ⭐ —SPECIALTY

1 small onion, chopped small
3 tablespoons olive oil
4 diced tomatoes
1 teaspoon sweet paprika
1/2 teaspoon each salt, pepper, and turmeric
1/2 cup water
1/2 cup fresh parsley, chopped, leaves only
4-6 chicken thighs

Add onions and olive oil to a pot, cook for 5 minutes, add diced tomatoes, stir together. Add all spices and mix well, add the water. Bring the pot to a boil, reduce and cook for 30 minutes. Place the chicken thighs right on the tomatoes, cover and cook on simmer for another 30 to 40 minutes, drizzle some of the sauce on the chicken thighs. This dish is usually cooked on charcoal where the pot has no water at all. Serve warm. This recipe yields about 5-6 servings.

MAMA'S TAGINE OF ARTICHOKE HEARTS FILLED WITH MEATBALLS & LEMON SAUCE — MOROCCO ⭐—SPECIALTY

1 tablespoon Lekama spice mix (see recipe in This and That category)
4 large garlic cloves minced
1 1/2 pounds ground beef or chicken
2-4 tablespoon olive oil
2 cup water
juice of 1 lemon
1 bag of frozen artichoke hearts

1/2 preserved lemon, sliced
1 large potato or 8 zucchini pieces shredded, or breadcrumbs (see
recipe in This and That category)
2-3 cups frozen green peas

In a mixing bowl add Lekama spice mix and ground meat, add
shredded vegetables or breadcrumbs, mix and set aside. Place olive oil
in a pan and add minced garlic, cook on low for 1 minute. Add the
water, mix. Add the lemon juice, cover the pot, and cook on low. Use
an ice cream scoop to make meat balls, you will get about 12-16 balls.
Add artichoke hearts to the sauce and place a meatball on each artichoke heart, if you have extra meatballs than artichoke hearts scatter
them in the pot. Add preserved lemons slices, scatter them all over the
pan. Do not add salt yet, remember that the preserved lemons are very
salty. Add the frozen green peas, scatter them everywhere in the pot.
Bring to a boil, cover and cook on simmer for 40-50 minutes. If you
would like to thicken the sauce more, remove the lid and let the steam
evaporate for a few more minutes. Serve warmly. This recipe yields
about 7 servings.

MAMA'S TAGINE OF CHICKEN, PRUNES & ONION JAM — MOROCCO 🌺 —IN MEMORY

2.5 pounds onions

1/4 cup vegetable oil (no olive oil in this dish)

1/4 cup raisins

1/4 cup walnuts

1 cup dry prunes

2 tablespoons vegetable oil for the onions (no olive oil in this dish)

1 teaspoon each cinnamon, ginger, sugar

1/2 teaspoon each nutmeg and turmeric

1/4 teaspoon salt

3 pounds chicken thighs

1 1/2 cups water

Mix all spices in a large bowl that can fit the chicken as well. Add the 1/4 cup vegetable oil, now mix oil and spices to blend well, add chicken thighs and brush well on all sides to get the spices' flavor everywhere on the chicken, set aside. Slice onions into thick slices and transfer to a pan. Add 2 tablespoons oil to the onions and cook 5 minutes and mix, add nuts and dried fruits to the onions and mix, finally add the chicken and mix. Cover and bring to a boil, reduce heat and cover, simmer for one hour. Every 10 minutes mix gently to blend flavors, keep the pot covered. Serve warm with plain rice, quinoa, pasta, or fresh salad. This recipe yields 5-7 servings.

MAMA'S TAGINE OF MEATBALLS IN RED SAUCE — MOROCCO, TUNISIA, SYRIA ⭐—SPECIALTY

1 large onion, chopped small
1/2 cup Italian parsley, leaves only
2 tablespoons cilantro chopped
1.5 pounds ground meat
1 tablespoon sweet paprika
1/2 teaspoon black pepper

1/2 teaspoon ground cinnamon

1/2 teaspoon ginger

1-1/2 teaspoon salt

2 teaspoon cumin

2 eggs or 1/2 cup breadcrumbs, or 1/2 cup shredded zucchini

For the sauce—

4 garlic cloves, minced

3 tablespoons olive oil

1/2 cup mixed cilantro, parsley, mint

2 teaspoons cumin

1/4-1/2 teaspoon black pepper

2 cups tomato sauce

1 cup beef broth

Optional pinch of cayenne pepper

Add chopped onions, chopped parsley, chopped cilantro, ground meat, sweet paprika, black pepper, cinnamon, ginger, salt, cumin, and eggs. Mix well to blend all spices and refrigerate for 30 minutes. Use an ice cream scoop to shape meatballs, you will get about 26 meatballs, set aside. Make the sauce—Add 3 tablespoons olive oil to a wide pan, add minced garlic, cook garlic for 1 minute, add cumin, black pepper, mixed herbs, cook another 1-2 minutes on low heat, mix constantly. Add tomato sauce, beef broth, cover, cook the sauce for 10 minutes. If using cayenne pepper add it at this step. Start adding the meatballs, gently shake the wide pan or Tagine to make sure the meatballs are all immersed in the sauce. Cover, cook on low for one hour. If the sauce is too liquid, you can uncover and cook it a little more to let steam evaporate. This is a very tasty dish, you can balance it nicely with plan rice, pasta, or fresh salad, serve warm.

MINA DEL CARNA — PASSOVER MEAT PIE — SPAIN, MOROCCO ⭐—SPECIALTY

12-14 matzah
1/2 cup olive oil

For the filling—
4 tablespoons vegetable oil
2 large onions, chopped
3 large garlic cloves, chopped
26 ounces ground beef
1 teaspoon each salt and black pepper
1/2 teaspoon cumin
4 eggs
3 tablespoons matzah flour
1 large potato, cooked and mashed
1/4 cup pine nuts
1/2 cup fresh parsley, chopped
3/4 cup chicken stock

Preheat oven to 350F (180C). Sprinkle water on all the matzah, wrap with clean towel and set aside. Add oil to a large pan, cook onions until golden brown. Add ground meat and garlic and cook to brown the meat. Add spices, mix to blend and cool down. Add eggs, Matzah flour, and mashed potatoes. Mix in the parsley and pine nuts. Brush a deep baking dish with oil, set several Matzah on the baking dish and on the side of the baking dish and brush Matzah with oil as well. Add half of the meat mixture, cover with Matzah and add another layer of meat. Now cover the meat mixture with the rest of the Matzah and brush with oil. Bake for 25 minutes until it is golden color. Drizzle the chicken stock on the meat pie and return it to the oven for another 10 minutes. Serve warmly. This recipe yields about 10 servings.

PASANJUN, SWEET PERSIAN MEATBALLS FROM ISPAHAN — IRAN

2.2 pounds ground meat (beef or mixed beef and dark chicken meat)
7 ounces walnuts coarsely chopped
1 large onion, chopped small
1 cup fresh Italian parsley, leaves only, chopped small
3 tablespoons breadcrumbs
1 tablespoon breadcrumbs
2-3 tablespoons olive oil
1 teaspoon each black pepper, cumin
1 teaspoon salt

For the sauce—
4 tablespoons vegetable oil
5 garlic cloves, chopped small
1 tablespoon fresh ginger, minced
11 ounces walnuts, coarsely chopped
2 cups hot water
1 teaspoon each salt and black pepper
1/2 cup Silan (date syrup)
1/4 cup pomegranate syrup

Preheat oven to 350F (180C). Brush a large baking dish with oil, set aside. Mix all meatball ingredients and use an ice cream scoop to shape meatballs, transfer meatballs to the baking dish. Bake meatballs for 12 minutes only. Make the sauce—Place oil in a wide pot, cook onions to brown. Add ginger and garlic, cook 1-2 minutes, add hot water, salt and pepper and bring to a boil. Reduce heat and simmer for one hour covered. Add Silan and pomegranate syrup and cook another 30 minutes on low heat. Serve meat balls warm and drizzle with sauce. Usually, this dish is served with plain rice. If you like sweet meatballs add more date syrup to your likeness. This dish yields about 7 servings.

SALMON IN RED SAUCE — FRIDAY NIGHT SHABBAT FISH — MOROCCO 🌺 —IN MEMORY

1/4 cup olive oil

5 garlic cloves, chopped

1/2 teaspoon cumin

2 teaspoon sweet or hot paprika

1/2-1 teaspoon salt

1/2 teaspoon black pepper

3-5 dry red ancho or California chili peppers

1/4 cup fresh cilantro

1 fresh tomato, diced

1 cup water

1 1/2 cups garbanzo beans, soaked overnight and cooked

2 pounds, salmon fish, sliced 1" x 3" size each slice

Place olive oil and garlic in a pan, cook for 1-2 minutes, add diced tomato, all spices, garbanzo beans, and half of the cilantro, cook on low heat for 1 minute to release flavors, add water, cover and bring to a boil. Reduce heat and cook for 25 minutes, add salmon slices to the pan and sprinkle with the rest of cilantro, bring to a boil, reduce heat and cook uncovered for 10-15 minutes, drizzle the liquids on the fish every few minutes. To serve—Place some garbanzo beans on a plate, add one chili pepper for flavoring and decoration, place salmon on the garbanzo beans and drizzle sauce on top, serve warm. This recipe yields 4-6 servings.

SAVORY FISH BALLS IN RED SAUCE — TUNISIA ⭐—SPECIALTY

For the fish balls—

1 pound 13 ounces white fish—cod, snapper, sea bass, mahi mahi

3 large garlic cloves, minced

1 large onion, chopped

2 tablespoons each Italian parsley and cilantro, both fresh and chopped

2 eggs

1/2 teaspoon salt

2 teaspoons Harissa (see recipe in This and That category)

2 teaspoons cumin

1/2 teaspoon grated orange zest

1 cup breadcrumbs or 4 slices stale bread

1/4 cup olive oil

For the tomato sauce—

3 garlic cloves, chopped

4 ounces tomato sauce

3 tablespoons olive oil

2 cups fish broth or water

2 large garlic cloves, minced

Salt and pepper to add after final tasting

Start by making the sauce—In a large pan that can fit all the meatballs add olive oil and garlic, cook on low for 1-2 minutes to release aroma. Add tomato sauce, cover and simmer for 5 minutes. Add water and bring sauce to a boil, cover, and simmer for 30 minutes. Transfer the fish balls ingredients to a large bowl, mix to blend well, refrigerate for 30 minutes. Use an ice cream scoop to form fish balls and place on a tray until all fish balls are ready. Transfer fish balls to the cooked tomato sauce, bring to a boil, reduce and simmer for 20 minutes. Serve on a bed of plain rice, couscous, or pasta. This recipe yields about 5 servings.

SPANISH SOPHRITO IS MOUTHWATERING DELIGHT — SPAIN ⏰ —QUICK & EASY

2 1/2 pounds chicken or beef for stew

7 large potatoes or 10 very small ones, cut to quarters

1/2 cup vegetable oil mixed with olive oil

1/2 teaspoon each salt and pepper

1 teaspoon Baharat spice mix (see recipe in the This and That category)

1/2 teaspoon turmeric

1/4 teaspoon saffron steeped in 1/4 cup hot water

1 whole fresh head of garlic, sliced in the middle to a half

1/3 cup boiling water

Place oil in a large heavy pot, cook the potatoes to brown a little. Transfer to a colander to drain but keep some of the oil in the pot. Add the meat pieces, cook to brown for a few minutes. Add spices, garlic, and boiling water, cover the pot and simmer for 2 hours. Keep checking that there is still some water, serve with a fresh salad, this recipe yields about 5-6 servings.

SWEET & SAVORY MEAT LOG FOR CHAMIN, SCHINA, DEFINA, CHULENT — FOREVER SHABBAT DISH 🌺 —IN MEMORY

1 cup walnuts or pecans
1 pound ground beef
1/4 cup vegetable oil (no olive oil)
1 teaspoon cinnamon
2 eggs
1/4 cup breadcrumbs
1 teaspoon black pepper
1/2 teaspoon ginger
1 teaspoon mace
3 tablespoons sugar
1/2 teaspoon nutmeg
1/4 teaspoon salt
1/4 cup raisins or dates
1 cookie bag

Place all ingredients for the sweet and spicy meat log in a food processor, mix for 3-5 minutes to blend all spices with the meat. Transfer to a cookie bag, shape like a log and roll all extra cookie bag to secure from leaking. Use a fork to poke several holes on the top part of the log. Set aside until ready to cook in the Shabbat chamin pot.

TAGINE OF CHICKEN, CELERY & LEMON SAUCE — MOROCCO, TUNISIA 🌺—IN MEMORY

4 garlic cloves sliced
1/4 cup olive oil
1/4 teaspoon mace
1/4 teaspoon saffron
1/2 teaspoon white pepper
2-3 preserved lemons, sliced (see recipe in This and That category)
2 tablespoons fresh parsley, leaves only, chopped
1 cup water
2-3 celery sticks for each serving, the size of 1" x 3"
8 pieces of chicken (legs, thighs, breast)
1/4 teaspoon salt (wait with the salt until final tasting)
juice of 1 lemon

If not using a large tagine, use a wide deep pot to accommodate all pieces of chicken. Place olive oil and garlic in a wide pan, cook for 1 minute on low heat, add all ingredients except chicken, celery sticks, water, and preserved lemons. Cook for 5 minutes on medium heat to release flavors, add all pieces of chicken and use a brush to coat all chicken with the spice mixture. Cover and cook to simmer for 30 minutes. Now add all celery sticks, place chicken on top of celery, add preserved lemons everywhere in the pan and add the water. Tilt the pan to mix all ingredients and bring to a boil. Reduce immediately to simmer and cook on low for 40 minutes. Check to see if more salt is needed but remember that the preserved lemons are very salty. Squeeze the juice of 1 fresh lemon on the chicken. This recipe yields about 7-8 servings.

TANZIA, SWEET CELEBRATION OF FRUITS & MEAT — MOROCCO ❀—IN MEMORY

5 apples, skin off, sliced to 1/2" think
1 cup dry apricots
1 cup dry prunes
Juice of 1 lemon
1 cup white wine vinegar
3 tablespoons honey
3 tablespoons vegetable oil (no olive oil)
1/2 teaspoon ginger
1 1/2 teaspoons cinnamon
1/2 teaspoon black pepper
1/2 teaspoon mace
1/4 teaspoon salt
6 pieces of chicken, thighs, legs
5 tablespoons honey for final step before baking

Place white wine vinegar in a large mixing bowl, add lemon juice, honey, cinnamon, ginger, black pepper, mace, and salt, mix well to blend the marinade. Soak all chicken pieces in the marinade for 30 minutes. Add apricots, prunes, soak in the marinade. Add oil to a metal pan that can go in the oven later, brown chicken on both sides. Add all apples and dry fruits to the pan. Drizzle the marinade on the chicken and fruits. Cover the pan, bring to a boil, simmer for 50 minutes. Right before serving drizzle the 5 tablespoons of honey on top and transfer to the oven, bake for 15 minutes only and serve warm. This recipe yields 6 servings.

TASTY LACHMA'AGUN, EASY MEAL — TURKEY ⏰—QUICK & EASY

2.2 pounds ground beef
1/2 bunch Italian parsley, chopped
2 tablespoons pomegranate syrup
2 tablespoons tomato paste
2 fresh tomatoes cubed
Juice of half lemon
1 teaspoon Baharat spice mix (see recipe in the This and That category)
1 large onion, chopped
1/2-1 teaspoon salt
4-6 pita bread

You will fall in love with this Turkish delight. Mix all ingredients except the pita bread to blend flavors. Refrigerate for 1/2-1 hour. Spread mixture on the pita bread. Bake in a preheated oven for about 10 minutes at 400F (200C). Be careful not to burn. Serve hot from the oven. This recipe yields about 4-6 servings.

TBIT — WHOLE CHICKEN STUFFED WITH RICE & VEGETABLE — IRAQ SHABBAT DISH 🍲—SLOW COOKER

For the crock pot—
1 whole chicken
2 tablespoons vegetable oil
2 onions, chopped
4 carrots cut in halves
2 zucchinis, cut in quarter
2 potatoes, cut in halves
1/2 teaspoon salt

2 tablespoons tomato paste

1 tablespoon Baharat spice mix (see recipe in This and That category)

1 teaspoon onion powder

2 cups chicken stock

1 teaspoon dry mint

1 cup long grain rice

2 cups water

For the stuffing—

1 1/2 cups long grain rice

4 small tomatoes, grated

1 large onion, chopped

2 large garlic cloves, minced

2 tablespoons Baharat spice mix (see recipe in This and That category)

2 teaspoons dry mint

1/4 cup vegetable oil

1/2-1 teaspoon salt

1/2 teaspoon black pepper

2 chicken wings (cut from the whole stuffed chicken)

1 egg

Start by making the stuffing—Place onions and oil in a large pan, cook with the 2 chicken wings to add flavors, brown the onions. Add the minced garlic cloves, rice, Baharat spice mix (see recipe), keep mixing while cooking on low. Add salt and pepper, dry mint, mix well, cook for 5 minutes. Add shredded tomatoes, cook for another 5 minutes. Add 2 cup chicken stock, mix. Now add 1 egg, mix, and let mixture cool down. Start filling the whole chicken with the rice filling (without the chicken wings). When you fill up the rice filling, secure the chicken- tie the extra chicken skin with cooking string if you have one. to secure the neckline of the chicken on the other side so that rice stuffing doesn't come out. Add 2 tablespoons oil to the same pan and place the stuffed chicken in it to brown all side of it, add the 2 chicken wings to the pan, cook just to brown. Place chicken in the crock pot, add vegetables and rice. Scrape all oil from the frying pan and add to the 2 cups of water, mix and pour over the rice in the crock pot. Add all other ingredients to the crock pot. Turn the crock pot on low and let it cook for 8 hours. This Iraqi Shabbat dish is another delicious comfort food to enjoy on a winter day. Serve warm from the crock pot, this dish yields about 7-8 servings.

YAFFA'S BRAIDED SALMON CHALLAH ⭐—SPECIALTY

5 pounds Salmon fish, one long fillet

bowl with cold water

1 tablespoon lemon juice

2 tablespoons capers

1/4 teaspoon chili flax

1 teaspoon fresh lemon zest
black pepper
1/2 teaspoon salt
juice from half lemon
1 tablespoon Dijon mustard
4 tablespoons olive oil
1 tablespoon fresh thyme
2 tablespoons dry dill

Preheat the oven to broil. Start by soaking the fish in a bowl with cold water and lemon juice, for 5 minutes. Use a sharp knife to slice the salmon lengthwise, to get 6 long pieces of salmon, set aside. Place capers, chili flax, lemon zest, black pepper, and salt in a bowl and mix. Add the lemon juice, Dijon mustard, olive oil, thyme, dill, and mix to blend flavors, set aside. Line up a baking tray with foil, transfer 3 pieces of salmon to the baking pan. Braid the same as if you are braiding a simple challah, set on one side of the baking pan. Now transfer the other 3 pieces of salmon to the baking pan and braid as a challah as well. The skin side of the salmon should be at the bottom side of the baking tray. Shape each salmon challah as in a circle shape to face each other and create a circle, tuck in the ends so that it will show as one connected salmon challah circle. Now brush the salmon challah with the capers sauce, brush everywhere, especially in all the folds and corners. Transfer to the oven and broil for 12 minutes only, remember that the salmon will cook for another 5 minutes after it is out of the oven. Serve warm or cold, this recipe yields about 6-8 servings.

YAFFA'S CHICKEN PASTIA, BESTILLA, BESTILE THE MOROCCAN FLAG DISH — MOROCCO ⭐—SPECIALTY

2 large onions, chopped small
1 cup vegetable oil

1/2 teaspoon each—salt, black pepper, ginger, cumin, sweet paprika, turmeric, cinnamon

1/4 teaspoon saffron threads in 1/4 cup water, soaked for 5 minutes

1 pound ground meat, beef or chicken

1/4 cup mix of fresh cilantro and fresh parsley

4-6 eggs

1/4 cup almonds

1 teaspoon sugar

1 teaspoon orange blossom

Powdered sugar and cinnamon to sprinkle after baking

Preheat oven to 350F (180C). Place chopped onions in a pan, add oil and caramelize, transfer to a separate bowl, to the same pan add oil, ground beef, salt, pepper, ginger, sweet paprika, cumin, cinnamon, 1/4 cup water, blend spices, about 5 minutes, transfer to a small bowl without cooked liquids, to the same pan that has the meat liquids add eggs and saffron liquid. Simmer, stir constantly, liquids will evaporate, and eggs will get the flavor of the meat and saffron liquids, eggs will become scrambled. Chop Almonds coarsely and transfer to a clean pan, add sugar and orange blossom water, and cook for 1-3 minutes, open filo dough package and take out one layer, cover filo dough with a clean towel. Fold filo layer into half, brush one filo dough with oil, transfer oiled filo dough to a baking dish that is large enough to cover the sides plus extra to cover the top, add about 1/4 cup of each bowl—first eggs mixture, second layer meat, sprinkle 2 tablespoon of cilantro parsley mixture on top of meat, third layer is onions and fourth layer is caramelized almonds. Cover baking dish with extra filo that is on the sides, brush extra filo with oil, take out another filo layer and fold into half, use as the final cover for pastia dish and tuck in the extra sides of filo into the sides of the dish, brush top layer of filo with oil and transfer to oven. Bake until golden brown, about 20 minutes. Let cool, when ready to serve sprinkle a little powdered sugar on top, sprinkle or decorate with cinnamon.

Serve warmly. This recipe yields 2 pastia dishes and can serve a total of 8 guests.

YAFFA'S CLASSIC SCHNITZEL, GLUTEN FREE BREADCRUMBS CRISPY, TASTY... & BAKED ⭐—SPECIALTY

1 tablespoon sesame seeds

1 cup gluten free breadcrumbs (or regular breadcrumbs)

1 cup gluten free flour (or all-purpose flour)

1/2 teaspoon dry dill

1 egg

1 teaspoon Dijon mustard

1 large chicken breast

olive oil for brushing

1/4 teaspoon each salt and pepper

olive oil spray

Preheat oven to 400F (200C). In a mixing bowl place flour, bread-crumbs, sesame seeds, dry dill, salt and pepper, mix well. In a separate bowl mix egg and mustard. Slice the chicken breast to no more than 1/4" thick, place schnitzel in the dry ingredients bowl and coat all sides. Transfer schnitzel to the egg mixture bowl and coat all sides, shake off excess liquids, transfer schnitzel again to the dry ingredients and coat all sides again. Line a baking pan with parchment paper and brush with a little olive oil. Place schnitzel on it and spray a little olive oil on top of schnitzel, bake in the oven for 5 minutes on each side, schnitzel should be golden brown from outside but soft inside, repeat with other pieces of chicken breast, serve warm with a slice of lemon. This recipe yields about 2-3 servings depending on how thick the schnitzel is.

YAFFA'S EGGS STUFFED WITH TASTY TUNA, HERBS & CAPERS

1 can of tuna
2 eggs, cooked, hard boiled, peeled
1 tablespoon fresh dill, chopped
1/4 teaspoon each salt and pepper
2 tablespoons cold press/extra virgin olive oil (optional, mayonnaise)
1 pickle, thinly sliced
1 tablespoon capers
1 tablespoon mustard or lemon juice

Mix all ingredients except for the eggs, refrigerate for 30 minutes for the flavors to blend. Use a sharp knife to divide the eggs to 2 halves. Remove the cooked egg yolk, use an ice cream scoop to take out one batch from the Tuna mix. Shape as a ball and place inside the boiled half egg. Serve on a platter decorated with parsley or lettuce leaves, serve cold. This recipe yields 4 servings.

YAFFA'S LIME DILL FISH WITH MUSHROOMS & CAPERS ⏰— QUICK & EASY

1 salmon fillet the size of 12" x 14"
1 cup olive oil
1 tablespoon fresh dill chopped
juice of 1 lime
1 tablespoon capers
1/2 teaspoon white pepper
1 cup mushrooms

Preheat oven to 400F (200C). Make the marinade first—In a small bowl place all ingredients, mix to blend well, set aside. Place the fish in a large bowl with 1 tablespoon lemon juice, soak the fish in it for 3-5 minutes, remove and transfer to a baking dish. Pour the marinade on the fish and brush fish to cover with the marinade and mushrooms. Bake for 12-15 minutes, remove from the oven and let rest for 10 minutes before serving, remember that the fish is still being cooked for another 5-7 minutes while resting. This recipe yields 5-6 servings.

YAFFA'S "MUST TRY" SHAKSHUKA — ISRAEL

2 cups "Matbucha tomato cooked salad" (see recipe in Salad's category)
2 eggs
1 green bell pepper or 2 jalapeño peppers
2 garlic cloves
2 tablespoons olive oil
1/4 teaspoon cumin (to get rid of the acidity)
1/4 teaspoon each salt and pepper

Nothing can be compared to a Shakshuka made of freshly cooked tomatoes which we devour in my home every week, but in my previous restaurant "Yaffa's Savory", we served this recipe, and customers devoured it and came all the way from the Rocky Mountains to enjoy this dish. In a small pan place green pepper or jalapeño and cook with nothing else added, let the pepper get char coaled a little with a few black spots on both side of it, this will add that smoky flavor to your Shakshuka, set aside. In a clean pan add the olive oil, garlic, "Matbucha" tomatoes, and cook for 3 minutes, add the cumin to balance the acidity, make 2 holes in the tomatoes and add the 2 eggs and the smoky pepper. Cover and cook on low to medium just until the eggs are cooked to your desired preference. Serve warm with crispy bread. This recipe yields 1-2 servings.

YAFFA'S QUICK & EASY QUINOA & TUNA CASSEROLE ⏰— QUICK & EASY

1 cup quinoa
2 tablespoons olive oil
1 large onion, chopped small
2 garlic cloves, minced
1 teaspoon turmeric
2 tablespoons fresh dill, chopped
1 can of tuna, drain water/oil
1/2 teaspoon each salt and pepper
2 cups water

Place olive oil and onion in a small pot, cook for 5 minutes to brown. Add garlic and turmeric, cook on low for 2 minutes to release aroma. Add the tuna, water, salt, pepper, and dill and bring to a boil, reduce to simmer, cover and cook for 20 minutes, this recipe yields about 3-4 servings.

YAFFA'S SALMON, ROOT VEGETABLE IN A DELIGHTFUL CREAMY SAUCE

For the fish—
5 salmon fillet slices
1/2 teaspoon each salt and pepper
1 tablespoon fresh thyme

For the creamy sauce—
2 tablespoons salted butter
2 tablespoons olive oil
1 tablespoon fresh thyme
2 leeks, white parts only, chopped
2 parsley roots, sliced
4 celery sticks, cut large
3 carrots, sliced small
4 large garlic cloves, minced
1/2 cup dry white wine
1 cup heavy cream
1/4 teaspoon each salt and pepper

Preheat the oven to 350F (180C). Make the creamy French sauce first. Place butter in a pan. Add olive oil, blend together on low heat. Add the fresh thyme to the pan, mix, cook to release aroma. Add all vegetables to the pan except the garlic. Cover and cook on low heat about 6-7 minutes. Add garlic to vegetables, gently mix, cook for 1 minute, set aside. For the fish use a pan that can go in the oven, oil the salmon pieces with olive oil, sprinkle the 1 tablespoon thyme on each salmon fillet and bake in the oven for 15 minutes. Add 1/2 cup white wine to the vegetables pan, cook for 3 minutes. Add the heavy cream, cook for 10 minutes, mix gently. Transfer the sauce to the fish pan, let the fish absorb the sauce. Serve warm with plain side dish to balance the rich salmon sauce. This recipe yields 5 servings.

YAFFA'S SAVORY MEATBALLS "HUGGED" IN EGGPLANT "WINGS"

10 ounces ground beef
1 1/2 teaspoons Lekama, Moroccan meatballs spice mix (see recipe in This and That category)
1/2 cup fresh parsley, leaves only
5 large garlic cloves, chopped
1 egg
2 very large eggplants
1 tablespoon chicken consume
2 cups chicken stock

In a bowl place Lekama spice mix (see recipe), chicken consume, parsley, garlic, and mix well to blend. Add 1 egg and whisk to blend. Add ground beef and mix to blend well. Let the meat mixture sit in the refrigerator for 30-60 minutes. Wash eggplants and slice each eggplant in a fan shape, each eggplant should have 6 openings to create the shape of a fan; keep the end intact. Place in a wide pan, add chicken stock. Divide the meat into 12 large oval meatballs, insert each meatball between the slices of the eggplant. Bring the eggplants to a boil, reduce and cook covered for 2 minutes. Occasionally, drizzle some of the liquids on the eggplants and the meatballs, the eggplant will release water, if the sauce has too many liquids in it, uncover and simmer a little more to thicken the sauce. Serve warmly. This recipe yields about 8-10 servings.

YAFFA'S SWEET & SAVORY BRISKET WITH BURGUNDY WINE, ORANGE SAUCE, & MUSHROOMS 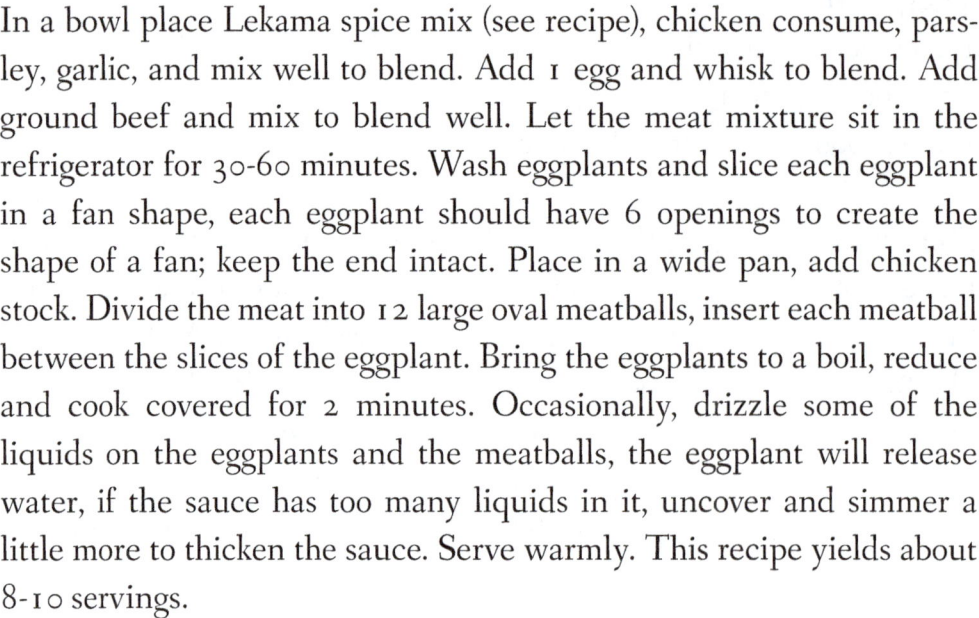—SLOW COOKER

1 bag of onion soup mix
1 2/3 cups burgundy wine

1/4 cup water

2 1/4 tablespoons flour

2 tablespoons dry thyme

1 tablespoon dry basil

1/3 cup orange marmalade

2 teaspoons fresh orange peel

2 1/4 teaspoons sugar

5 garlic cloves, minced

1/2 teaspoon black pepper

4 pounds beef brisket

1 1/2 pounds fresh mushrooms, sliced

Preheat oven to 275F (135C). In a large bowl mix the onion soup mix, wine, water, and flour, mix well. Add thyme, basil, and mix well, add orange marmalade and blend in, add orange peel, sugar, garlic and mix well, add pepper and mix again. Transfer the mixture to a deep baking dish, ceramic or glass, add brisket meat and cover with mushrooms. Bake uncovered for 4 hours until it is well done, if the sauce is too liquid you can transfer the sauce to a small pot and simmer on the stove until desired consistency is reached. This recipe yields 7-8 servings.

YAFFA'S THANKSGIVING TURKEY... SEPHARDIC STYLE ⭐— SPECIALTY

1 1/2 cups Italian parsley, chopped

3 tablespoons oregano

3 tablespoons thyme

2 tablespoons rosemary

1/2 teaspoon black pepper

1 teaspoon coriander

2 teaspoons sweet paprika

12 garlic cloves, sliced

1 teaspoon chicken consume

1/2 cup olive oil

25-pound turkey, thawed

20 toothpicks, in case you need more than 1

1 teaspoon salt

cooking string

Preheat oven to 300F (150C). Place all herbs in a small bowl, add olive oil, garlic, black pepper, coriander, salt, paprika, and chicken consume, mix to blend. Very gently separate the turkey skin from the meat, try not to make holes in the skin, as much as you can. The more you can separate the skin from the meat the better; the turkey will be moist and seasoned. I insert my hands to easily separate the skin, and scissors can help with that too. Usually, the breast side will be more challenging but do the best you can. Now use your hand to grab some of the herbs/oil mixture and insert it in between the turkey skin and the meat. This will help to seal the meat from drying out, use all the herbs mixture and if you have some extra, brush it on the turkey skin as well.

Use cooking string to tie the turkey legs together. Turkey should be breast side up. When the legs are tied, add one more time to add the back to the legs, now the whole body is tied up. Take 2 sides of the skin and secure them with a toothpick to cover the meat as much as possible, drizzle all remaining marinade on the turkey. Place turkey on the roasting pan and place in the oven, bake for 4-4.5 hours depending on your oven and the turkey size. Every 30 minutes drizzle the oils and liquids that drip back on the turkey for flavoring. This recipe yields for about 10 servings.

To complete your meal, see YAFFA'S THANKSGIVING STUFFING... SEPHARDIC STYLE and YAFFA'S THANKS-GIVING GRAVY... SEPHARDIC STYLE in the Vegetables & Side Dishes section.

YAFFA'S TUNA BURGER FOR THE SOUL — ISRAEL ⭐— SPECIALTY

2 small cans of tuna in water (5.4 ounces each)
2 tablespoons fresh dill
2 tablespoons fresh thyme
1/2 teaspoon each salt and pepper

1 tablespoon chia seeds or flax seeds for binding
1 small potato, cooked, skin peeled off
1 cup zucchini, shredded
1 egg
1/2 cup fresh parsley, chopped, leaves only
Olive oil for brushing if baking
Vegetable oil if frying

Preheat oven to 375F (190C). If baking, squeeze any water from the tuna fish. Add all the ingredients except the oils to a large mixing bowl, mix well, make sure that all the tuna fish crumbles evenly and is well mixed with everything else. Line a tray with parchment paper. Grab about a 1/2 cup of the mixture and shape like a patty. Repeat with all the tuna mix. Each patty should be no more than 1/2" thick. If baking, brush the patties with a little olive oil on both sides, transfer to the oven and bake 7-10 minutes on both sides to a golden brown. If frying, heat vegetable oil in a pan, fry about 5-6 minutes on each side to golden brown, transfer to a colander to drain excess oil. Serve warm with a half lemon. This recipe yields about 8 tuna patties.

Breads & Rolls

HELPFUL HINTS

- When baking bread, a small dish of water in the oven will keep the crust from getting too hard or brown.
- Use shortening, not margarine or oil, to grease pans when baking bread. Margarine and oil absorb more readily into the dough.
- To make self-rising flour, mix 4 cups flour, 2 teaspoons salt, and 2 tablespoons baking powder. Store in a tightly covered container.
- One scant tablespoon of bulk yeast is equal to one packet of yeast.
- Hot water kills yeast. One way to test for the correct temperature is to pour the water over your wrist. If you cannot feel hot or cold, the temperature is just right.
- When in doubt, always sift flour before measuring.
- Use bread flour for baking heavier breads, such as mixed grain, pizza doughs, bagels, etc.
- When baking in a glass pan, reduce the oven temperature by 25°.

- When baking bread, you can achieve a finer texture if you use milk. Water makes a coarser bread.
- Fill an empty saltshaker with flour to quickly and easily dust a bread pan or work surface.
- For successful quick breads, do not overmix the dough. Mix only until combined. An overmixed batter creates tough and rubbery muffins, biscuits, and quick breads.
- Muffins can be eaten warm. Most other quick breads taste better the next day. Nut breads are better if stored 24 hours before serving.
- Nuts, shelled and unshelled, keep best and longest when stored in the freezer. Unshelled nuts crack more easily when frozen. Nuts can be used directly from the freezer.
- Enhance the flavor of nuts, such as almonds, walnuts, and pecans, by toasting them before using in recipes. Place nuts on a baking sheet and bake at 300°F for 5-8 minutes or until slightly browned.
- Overripe bananas can be frozen until it's time to bake. Store them unpeeled in a plastic bag.
- The freshness of eggs can be tested by placing them in a large bowl of cold water; if they float, do not use them.

AFTER PASSOVER KEY CHALLAH ⭐—SPECIALTY

1 1/4 cups water
1 tablespoon dry yeast
3 tablespoons sugar
3 tablespoons vegetable oil
1 pound 10 ounces all-purpose flour
1 1/2 teaspoon salt
1 egg for brushing

For decoration—
sesame seeds, olives, capers, cherry tomatoes, rosemary

Preheat oven to 350F (180C). Place water, dry yeast, sugar, oil and flour in a mixer, mix for 3-4 minutes. Add salt and mix for 10 minutes. This dough will be very elastic and easy to work with. Sprinkle some flour in a bowl then transfer dough to the bowl and top with more flour. Cover the dough with a clean towel and let rest for 30 minutes. Divide dough to 6 parts, make a simple braiding with the first 3 parts, close the braid to create a circle challah. Transfer to a baking pan lined with parchment paper. Braid the other 3 parts to make a challah and connect to the circle challah to create the shape of a key. Twist the end of the long challah to give it a little angled end to help shape it like a key. Brush with egg, decorate with your choice of decoration, bake for 30 minutes. Let cool down and cover with a clean towel. Add 3 or 4 small manikins filled with horseradish, harissa— (see recipe in This and That category) hummus, or any dip of your choice and place them inside the circle challah. Serve at room temperature.

CRANBERRY ORANGE GLUTEN FREE TAHINI BREAD

4 eggs
1/4 teaspoon salt
2 1/2 tablespoons syrup such as maple, agave, honey, dates
1 tablespoon vegetable oil (no olive oil in this one)
1 teaspoon baking soda
1/2 cup chopped walnuts
1/2 cup dry cranberries
1 teaspoon orange extract
1 tablespoon orange zest

Preheat oven to 375F (190C). Add all ingredients to a mixing bowl except walnuts and cranberries, whisk well. Fold in walnuts and cranberries, 1 cup tahini (not roasted sesame seeds). Transfer to a bread baking dish lined with parchment paper, pour batter in baking dish, bake for 30-45 minutes until golden brown. Let it cool down, serve with jam or cheese spread. Store in refrigerator. This amount yields 1 loaf of bread.

CRISPY FOCACCIA, IS SOOOO TASTY & CRISPY ⏰—QUICK & EASY

17 ounces all-purpose flour
1 cup slightly warm water
1 medium potato, cooked andmashed
2 tablespoons olive oil
1 1/2 tablespoons dry yeast
1 1/2 teaspoons salt
1/2 cup green or black olives
2/3 teaspoon sea salt
2 tablespoons olive oil

2 tablespoons fresh thyme

Preheat oven to 425F (218C). In a mixer place 1/2 cup flour, dry yeast, 1/2 cup water. Mix until blended. Cover and let rise for 20 minutes. Add the rest of the flour, mashed potato, olive oil, and 1/2 cup water, mix well. Add olive oil and salt. Brush a bowl with a little olive oil. Place dough in the bowl and cover dough with olive oil. Cover bowl with clear plastic and let rise to double the size. Separate fresh thyme leaves from stems, slice the olives, set aside. Dip your finger in water, press your finger to create some holes in the dough while stretching the dough to open. Flat dough should be the size of 16" x 16". Cover and let rest for 15 minutes. Sprinkle thyme, olives, and sea salt if added. Drizzle 2 tablespoons olive oil on top of the dough. Cover and let rest for 1 hour. Bake for 20-25 minutes.

MINI CHALLAH BREADS — ISRAEL

2 teaspoons dry yeast
1/2 cup warm water
1 teaspoon honey
1 egg yolk
1/3 cup oil
4 cups all-purpose flour
1 1/4 teaspoon salt
1 egg for brushing
sesame seeds to sprinkle
honey to brush if desired
poppy seeds if desired

Preheat oven to 350F (180C). In a mixer bowl add water, honey, and dry yeast, let sit 3-5 minutes. Add egg yolk and mix well. Add the rest of the eggs and mix. Add oil, mix well. Add flour and mix on low (#1) for 23 minutes. Now add salt. Flour a bowl with a little flour and place the dough inside, sprinkle flour on top of the dough as well. Cover with clear plastic and let rise for 1.5 hours. Remove clear plastic and knead the dough to remove some of the air pockets. Dough should be soft and easy to work with. Let the dough sit another 15 minutes. Divide dough to 6 parts, braid the dough to get a small challah and brush with the egg. Sprinkle sesame seeds or poppy seeds if desired. Let the mini challah rest another 40 minutes before baking. Bake until golden brown, about 25-30 minutes or until golden brown. Take out of the oven, let cool and cover with clean towel.

PITA BREAD "AL BABOOR" STYLE (FOR KEBABS) ⏰—QUICK & EASY

2.2 pounds all-purpose flour
1 teaspoon salt
1/2 teaspoon dry yeast
4 cups water
2 tablespoons sesame seeds, fennel seeds

Preheat oven to 400F (200C). Mix flour, dry yeast, water, and salt. Dough will be thicker than normal, that is OK. Cover with a towel and let rise for one hour. Knead the dough for 8-10 minutes, make small balls, about 7 ounces each, transfer to a floured surface, cover with towel and let rest for 25 minutes. Before baking, roll out each dough to open to a 7" diameter. When the kebabs are ready to go in the oven, cover the kebabs with this pita, sprinkle sesame seeds or fennel seeds or both and bake together for 10-15 minutes. This recipe yields about 6 servings.

PULL APART & IRRESISTIBLE, SHAVUOT SPINACH & CHEESE CHALLAH ⭐—SPECIALTY

1 pound 10 ounces all-purpose flour

1 tablespoon dry yeast

4 tablespoons honey

1 1/4 cups water

4 tablespoons olive oil

1 teaspoon salt

For the filling—

1 cup defrosted spinach leaves, chopped

1 cup fresh spinach leaves, chopped

1 cup mozzarella, shredded

1 cup goat cheese, shredded

1/2 cup plain cream cheese

Preheat oven to 400F (200C). In a mixer add flour, yeast, and honey, add water, olive oil and mix 3-4 minutes. Add salt and mix on low for 10 minutes. Dough should be sticky and airy but still great to work with. Sprinkle a bowl with flour, add the dough and sprinkle more flour on top. Cover with a towel and let rest for 45 minutes. Squeeze the defrosted spinach leaves, place in a bowl, add the fresh spinach, mozzarella, goat cheese, and plain cream cheese. Divide the dough into 2 parts, add half of the cheese mixture and half of the spinach mixture. Use a sharp knife to slice the dough into 2 long parts, now divide each long part to 4 equal parts, fold a little, while still showing the filling and place the 4 parts in a round baking dish. make sure that every part is very close to the next one to create round pieces of fun challah shape. Repeat with the second half of dough and the filling. Brush the top surface with egg and transfer to the oven. Bake for 35-40 minutes. This is a great surprise treat for the Shavuot holiday table, this recipe yields one large round challah.

PURIM BREAD — KUMERA DEL PURIM, BUYOZO DE NEGOLA, SPAIN, MOROCCO 🌺—IN MEMORY

2.2 pounds flour

3 eggs and 1 for brushing

1/2 cup vegetable oil

1 tablespoon sesame seeds

1 cup chopped almonds

2/3 cup raisins

1 tablespoon anise seeds

1 1/2 tablespoons dry yeast

1/4 teaspoon salt

2 1/4 cups lukewarm water

1 cup sugar

6-8 hardboiled eggs

1/2 cup almonds, sliced, for decoration

Preheat oven to 350F (180C). Place flour and 3 eggs in a mixer, add all other ingredients except the egg for brushing and sliced almond to use for decoration. Mix on low (#1) for 10 minutes. Remove dough from the mixer and transfer to a dough proofing bowl and let rise for 2 hours. Divide dough to as many breads you would like to make, this amount made 6 breads for me. The dough will be sticky but it's normal, the dough will be soft, light with a lot of air pockets. Sprinkle some flour on the surface, roll to open one part of the dough and depending on how you would like to design your bread, I made each bread into a challah shape and added one hardboiled egg in the middle. Brush the bread, sprinkle some sliced almond on top and cover with towel for 10-15 minutes. Bake until golden brown, let cool a little, cover with clean towel and repeat with all other batches of dough. The tradition is that the youngest one in the family gets the first bread. This is a delightful sweet and savory holiday Purim bread. This recipe yields about 6 medium round breads.

ROSH HASHANA DELIGHT — CRANBERRY ORANGE CHALLAH ⭐—SPECIALTY

1/3 cup vegetable oil

3 tablespoons honey

2 tablespoons dry yeast

2 eggs

1 egg

1/2 cup freshly squeezed orange juice

1 teaspoon orange extract

1 tablespoon orange zest

1/2 cup dry cranberries

4 cups all-purpose flour
1 teaspoon salt
1 egg for decoration

Preheat oven to 350F (180C). In a mixer bowl place orange juice, yeast, honey, and mix. Crack 1 egg and add only the egg yolk to the yeast mixture, reserve the egg white for brushing. Add 2 more eggs, oil and mix well, add orange zest, orange extract, and dry cranberries, start the mixer on low. Add flour and mix for 3 minutes, add salt and mix for 10 minutes. Oil a mixing bowl with vegetable oil and transfer dough to the bowl, turn the dough around to make sure all sides of the dough are oiled. Cover dough with clear plastic, let rise for 1 1/2 hours. Punch dough with your fingers to get some of the air out and improve texture. Let rest for 15 minutes. Line a baking pan with parchment paper, sprinkle with flour. Divide dough into 2 parts, braid your challah the way you would like and transfer to baking pan. Cover baking pan with a clean towel and let rest for 40 minutes. Bake for 30-40 or until golden brown. Let challah cool down and cover with a towel. Serve at room temperature, this recipe yields one large round challah or 6 mini challahs.

THANKSGIVING PUMPKIN DINNER ROLLS

1/2 cup slightly warm milk
2 teaspoons dry yeast
1/2 cup pumpkin purée
3 tablespoons unsalted butter, room temperature
1 egg
1/4 cup brown sugar
2 1/2 cups flour
1/4-1/2 teaspoon salt
8 cooking strings 16" long each

3 tablespoons vegetable oil in a bowl

1 egg for brushing

Preheat oven to 350F (180C). Turn the mixer on low, add ingredients in this order while the mixer is mixing—slightly warm milk, dry yeast, pumpkin purée, unsalted butter, 1 egg, brown sugar, flour, mix for 4 minutes. Now add salt, mix for 8-10 minutes. Dough should be sticky. Cover dough and let rise for 1 hour. Divide dough to 8 equal parts, roll each part to form a ball, sprinkle with flour and cover with clean towel. Take out one dough ball, keep all other balls covered with a towel. Dip all strings in vegetable oil bowl. Loosely wrap the string around the dough ball 6 times to create the shape of a pumpkin. The pumpkin will rise so make sure that the string is loose. Repeat with all dough balls to create 8 pumpkin rolls. Cover dough and let rise for one hour, brush with egg, bake for about 20 minutes. Let cool down and serve at room temperature.

YAFFA'S AWESOME PITA BREAD ⭐—SPECIALTY

2.2 pounds all-purpose flour

2 tablespoons dry yeast

1 tablespoon sugar

2 tablespoons olive oil

3 cups warm water

1 tablespoon salt

Preheat oven to 500F (260C). Place flour in a mixing bowl, add sugar and dry yeast, mix on low. Add water, oil and mix for 3 minutes, add salt and mix for 10 minutes. Transfer the dough to a floured bowl, sprinkle with a little salt, cover with a clear plastic, let it sit for 1 hour. The dough will rise more than double of the size which is normal. Set a small bowl with water for the sticky hands, line a baking pan with parchment paper and generously sprinkle with flour. Grab small ball from the flour, shape it like a small ball and place it right on the floured baking pan. Dip your hands in the water whenever they are sticky with dough. Repeat with all the rest of the flour. Each ball should be the size of 1/2 to 2/3 of a cup. Get another baking pan and sprinkle it generously with flour. Sprinkle your work area as well with flour, remember that the dough is very sticky. Transfer one dough ball to the floured working area and use a rolling pin to stretch it a little, creating a size of about 7" diameter. Transfer it to the empty baking pan that you floured. Repeat with one or 2 more dough balls to create 2 more circles of dough, now you are ready to place them in the oven. Make sure that your oven is very hot, bake for 4-5 minutes only. Transfer to a clean towel, let cool down. Repeat with the rest of the dough balls. Slice the top of a pita bread to see the inside pocket, let it air a minute before filling it up with your favorite choice of filling, this recipe yields between 10-12 Pita breads.

YAFFA'S FAMOUS PASSOVER DINNER ROLLS

6 large eggs
1/2 teaspoon lemon zest
2 cups mineral water
2 cups matzah meal
1/2 cup sunflower oil
1 teaspoon salt
pinch of black pepper

Preheat oven to 400F (200C). In a saucepan add mineral water, oil, lemon zest, salt and pepper. Bring to a boil and immediately remove from heat. In a separate bowl crack the eggs, mix well, add to the pot and mix well. Add matzah meal gradually while mixing constantly. Transfer to cupcake baking pan and bake at 400F

(200C) for 40-50 minutes. Let cool before serving. This amount yields 12 dinner rolls.

YAFFA'S GLUTEN FREE TAHINI BREAD ⏰—QUICK & EASY

4 eggs
1 cup raw tahini sesame paste (not roasted sesame)
2 tablespoons syrup such as maple, honey, dates
1 tablespoon olive oil
1/2-3/4 teaspoon salt
1 teaspoon baking soda
1/2 cup chopped walnuts (optional)
1/2 cup pumpkin seeds (optional)
2-3 tablespoons sesame seeds
1 tablespoon dry herbs oregano, thyme, dill, or marjoram (optional)

Preheat oven to 375F (190C). Add eggs, tahini paste, syrup, oil, baking soda, to a mixing bowl, add herbs if using, whisk to blend well. Line a bread baking dish with parchment paper, transfer batter to a bread baking dish, sprinkle chopped walnuts and pumpkin seeds on top. Bake until bread rises and is golden brown. Let cool down. Serve at room temperature. This amount yields 1 loaf of bread.

YAFFA'S GLUTEN FREE TASTY HERBS BREAD ⭐—SPECIALTY

1/2 cup raw tahini (not roasted)
3 tablespoons sun-dried tomatoes, chopped
2 tablespoons olive oil
1/4 cup plain Greek yogurt
1/4 cup almond flour
1/4 cup tapioca
1/4 cup corn flour or corn meal

1/2 cup mixture of oregano, basil, and rosemary
3 eggs
1/2 teaspoon salt

Preheat oven to 350F (180C). Mix eggs, add tahini, and Greek yogurt. In a separate bowl place sun-dried tomato, chopped herbs, almond flour, tapioca flour, and corn flour, gently fold in the flours to mix with the sun-dried tomatoes, this way the sun-dried tomatoes will not sink in the bread during the baking, add flours' mixture into the egg's mixture, add salt and baking soda, fold it in to mix gently. Line a bread baking dish with parchment paper and brush with the olive oil, pour in the batter, level it a little, bake for 40 minutes or until golden color, let cool down for a while before slicing.

YAFFA'S HOMEMADE PASSOVER MATZAH ⭐—SPECIALTY

2 1/2 cups flour
1/2 cup water
2 tablespoons olive oil
1/2 teaspoon salt
Optional—dry herbs to flavor your matzah

Preheat a frying pan on the stove, do not add oil to it. Add salt and olive oil to a bowl, add 1/2 of the water, you might not need all the water. Use your hands or a mixer to knead the dough. The dough should be soft and easy to work with. Use a rolling pin to open or stretch the dough with your fingers. If dough is sticky, add some flour. The dough should be very thin. Use a fork to poke holes in the dough. This recipe yields 4 large matzah. The matzah can be either square or circle. Heat up a frying pan without oil. Cook the matzah on medium high for 1-2 minutes and flip the matzah to the other side. You have only 18 minutes to cook or bake the matzah so that it doesn't rise to be kosher for Passover. The matzah will get a few brown spots which is normal. Transfer to a clean towel and let cool down. This recipe yields between 8-12 matzah.

YAFFA'S OLIVE BREAD, TASTY & CRISPY ⭐—SPECIALTY

3 cups all-purpose flour
1/2 teaspoon dry yeast
1 1/2 cups water
1 tablespoon olive oil
1 teaspoon fresh thyme
1 teaspoon lemon zest
1 cup olives, green or black, sliced
1 1/2 teaspoons salt

Preheat oven to 375F (190C). Add dry yeast and water to a mixer, let sit for 3 minutes, add olive oil, lemon zest, thyme, flour, sliced olives, and mix for 10 minutes, the dough should be very soft but elastic and good to work with. Brush a bowl with olive oil, transfer the dough and turn dough to other side to cover it all with olive oil. Transfer the dough to a work surface and knead the dough to form a bread shape in the size of 4" x 8-9" long. Line a bread baking dish with parchment paper, cover with clear plastic and let sit for 1 hour. Flour the top of the dough with some flour and bake in the oven until golden brown, about 30-40 minutes. Transfer to a clean towel and let cool before slicing. Bread will be very crispy. This recipe yields one large rectangle bread.

YAFFA'S TASTY GARLIC CHALLAH ⭐—SPECIALTY

1/2 cup warm water
1 tablespoon dry yeast
1/4 cup honey

1 egg yolk

2 eggs

1/3 cup vegetable oil

1 1/4 teaspoons salt

3 3/4 cups all-purpose flour

For the garlic spread—

1 tablespoon olive oil

1/2 teaspoon salt

1 large garlic clove, minced

1/4 cup green onions, chopped small

Preheat oven to 350F (180C). Place water and dry yeast in a mixer, mix and let sit for 3 minutes. Add honey, mix and let sit for another 2 minutes. Add 1 egg yolk and mix, add 2 more eggs, oil and salt, mix well. Add flour and mix for 10 minutes. Sprinkle a bowl with some flour, transfer the dough, and top with more flour. Cover with clear plastic, let dough rise for 1.5 hours. In the meantime, mix all garlic spread ingredients, set aside. Roll dough to open to 1/2" thick, divide dough to 2 parts to make 2 challahs. Divide each dough to 3 equal parts, brush with 1/2 of the garlic spread on all 3 parts, reserve the rest for the second challah. Fold each 1/3 dough to create a log filled with garlic spread. Transfer all 3 garlic logs to a baking pan before braiding to a challah. Now braid the 3 logs to make one challah, tuck the 2 ends underneath to secure the challah's 2 ends. Brush challah with the egg white and sprinkle sesame seeds. Cover the challah with a clean towel and let rest for 40 minutes, then bake for 20 minutes. Cover loosely with aluminum foil and bake another 20 minutes. Let challah cool down, serve at room temperature. This recipe yields one large round Garlic challah.

DESSERTS

HELPFUL HINTS

- Keep eggs at room temperature to create greater volume when whipping egg whites for meringue.
- Pie dough can be frozen. Roll dough out between sheets of plastic wrap, stack in a pizza box, and keep the box in the freezer. Defrost the fridge and use as needed. Use within 2 months.
- Place your pie plate on a cake stand when ready to flute the edges of the pie. The cake stand will make it easier to turn the pie plate, and you won't have to stoop over.
- When making decorative pie edges, use a spoon for the scalloped edge. Use a fork to make crosshatched and herringbone patterns.
- When cutting butter into flour for pastry dough, the process is easier if you cut the butter into small pieces before adding it to the flour.
- Pumpkin and other custard-style pies are done when they jiggle slightly in the middle. Fruit pies are done when the pastry is golden, juices bubble, and fruit is tender.

- Keep the cake plate clean while frosting by sliding 6-inch strips of waxed paper under each side of the cake. Once the cake is frosted and the frosting is set, pull the strips away, leaving a clean plate.
- Create a quick decorating tube to ice your cake with chocolate. Put chocolate in a heat-safe, zipper-lock plastic bag. Immerse it in simmering water until the chocolate is melted. Snip off the tip of one corner and squeeze the chocolate out of the bag.
- Achieve professionally decorated cakes with a silky, molten look by blow-drying the frosting with a hair dryer until the frosting melts slightly.
- To ensure that you have equal amounts of batter in each pan when making a layered cake, use a kitchen scale to measure the weight.
- Prevent cracking in your cheesecake by placing a shallow pan of hot water on the bottom oven rack and keeping the oven door shut during baking.
- A cheesecake needs several hours to chill and set.
- For a perfectly cut cheesecake, dip the knife into hot water and clean it after each cut. You can also hold a length of dental floss taut and pull it down through the cheesecake to make a clean cut across the diameter of the cake.

APPLE TORT FOR EVERY OCCASION ⏰—QUICK & EASY

For the dough—
1 stick of unsalted cold butter (113 grams), shredded
1 1/2 cups all-purpose flour
1 egg yolk
1/2 cup sugar
1 teaspoon vanilla extract

For the apple filling—
10 medium apples, cored, skin peeled, sliced
3 egg yolks
3 egg whites
1/2 cup sugar
1/2 cup flour
1 teaspoon lemon zest
1 teaspoon cinnamon
1/4 cup sugar
pinch of salt

Preheat the oven to 350F (180C). Place in a mixer all ingredients for the dough, mix on low speed for 5 minutes, dough should be soft, if it needs add 1-2 tablespoons ice water to help soften and mix another 2 minutes. Transfer the dough to a baking pan, use your fingers to help spread the dough evenly. Make sure to cover the sides of the baking pan with the dough. Poke the dough with a fork, about 15 times, this will help the dough air and will not rise. Bake for 15 minutes, remove and set aside. Add 1 tablespoon lemon juice to an ice water filled bowl, place all apples in the bowl. Grate/shred the apples, place apples in a bowl to start releasing juice and refrigerate. In a small bowl mix cinnamon, lemon zest, and sugar, set aside. Place 3 egg whites and 1/2 cup sugar in the mixer and whip to a stiff cream. In a separate bowl mix the 3 egg yolks. Combine the egg yolks and egg whites by gently folding, try not to break the air pockets that the egg whites created. Add the 1/2 cup flour to the egg whites and gently fold it in the egg white's mixture. To assemble the cake—Squeeze the apple juice from the shredded apples, divide the shredded apples into 1/3 and 2/3. Add the 2/3 batch to the baked dough. Spread apples evenly on the baked dough. Sprinkle the cinnamon mix on the apples, now add 1/3 of shredded apples to the egg white's mixture and evenly spread on top. Bake the apple tort for about one hour, let sit for 10 minutes before slicing. This recipe yields about 12 servings.

BEIRUT NIGHTS PUDDING — LEBANON 🍎—VEGETARIAN

2 tablespoons vegetable oil

For the Semolina layer—
3 3/4 cups milk—whole milk is best
1/3 cup unsalted butter
pinch of salt
2 tablespoons sugar
1 teaspoon vanilla extract
1 cup semolina
1 teaspoon orange blossom

For the pistachio cream—
2 cups heavy cream, very cold
3 tablespoons instant vanilla pudding
3 tablespoons pistachio, ground to powder
2 tablespoons powder sugar

For the syrup—

9 ounces sugar

1 cup water

zest of 1 lemon

juice of half lemon

1/2 teaspoon orange blossom

3.5 ounces pistachio, coarsely chopped

Use a brush to oil a long rectangle baking dish. In a pot place the milk, butter, salt, sugar, vanilla extract, and bring to a boil. Reduce immediately and gradually add semolina, while mixing constantly. The mixture will start thickening, do not stop mixing, this will make sure that you are scraping the bottom of the pot. Let the semolina mixture cool down. Add the orange blossom and mix to blend. In a mixer add the heavy whipping cream, powdered sugar, and instant vanilla pudding, ground pistachios, whip to get a pistachio whip cream and refrigerate. While the semolina is being cooled down make the syrup. In a small pot place the sugar, water, lemon zest, and lemon juice and bring to a boil, reduce and cook for about 10 minutes to thicken a little. When the syrup is ready add 1/2 teaspoon of orange blossom, mix to blend. To assemble—add the pistachio cream right on top of the semolina cream, spread it evenly on the semolina cream. Refrigerate for 4 hours. When you are ready to serve the pudding, transfer one piece of the pudding to a small plate, drizzle the syrup on it and top with some coarsely chopped pistachios. This dessert yields about 10-12 servings. If you use plant-based butter, milk, and whipped cream you can make this dessert vegan.

BLUEBERRIES CHEESECAKE — ISRAEL ⏰—QUICK & EASY

For the dough—

2 cups flour

2 tablespoons unsalted butter

3 tablespoons powdered sugar
1/2 tablespoon baking powder
3 tablespoons vegetable oil
1/2 teaspoon vanilla extract

For the filling—
1.2 pounds cottage cheese
1 pound sour cream
2 1/2 cups milk
1 teaspoon orange extract
1 tablespoon orange zest
4 eggs
1 1/4 cups sugar
6 tablespoons corn starch
1 cup fresh blueberries

Preheat oven to 335F (160C). Place all dough ingredients in a mixer on a low speed, just enough to create a soft dough. Transfer dough to a baking dish, use your fingers to spread the dough evenly including the sides and bake for 15 minutes, set aside. In a mixer place all filling ingredients and mix well, scrape sides of the mixer, mix again. Add 2 cups of fresh blueberries, level up the blueberries and the cream. Bake for 1 1/2 hours. Let cool in the pan for one hour before slicing. Chill in the refrigerator. This recipe yields about 10 servings.

EASY CHOCOLATE CAKE — MID WEEK DESSERT ⏰—QUICK & EASY

4 egg whites
1/4 cup sugar for egg whites
1/3 cup and 1 tablespoon vegetable oil
4 egg yolks

1/4 cup sugar for egg yolks

3 tablespoons cocoa powder

1 tablespoon instant coffee powder

1 1/2 cups flour

1 teaspoon baking soda

For the syrup—

1/2 cup sugar

1/2 cup warm water

1 teaspoon instant coffee

1 teaspoon rum

For the chocolate ganache—

1 cup heavy whipping cream

3 ounces chocolate chips

Preheat oven to 350F (180C). Place egg whites, 1/4 cup sugar, and whip the egg whites to a stiff cream. In a separate bowl mix the egg yolks with 1/4 cup sugar, cocoa powder, instant coffee, 1/2 cup water, 1/3 cup and 1 tablespoon vegetable oil, 1/2 teaspoon baking powder, and the flour, mix to blend to a smooth batter. Gently fold in 1/4 cup of the egg whites with the cocoa mixture. Now fold in the rest of the egg whites with the cocoa mixture. Brush a baking pan with a little oil or spray with nonstick spray, pour the batter into the baking pan, bake for about 25-30 minutes. Insert a toothpick to check if the cake is ready. If the toothpick is wet, return the cake to the oven for another 5 minutes. Cake should be completely cold before slicing it. Slice the cake in the middle to create 2 layers, let cool. Make the syrup—Bring all syrup ingredients to a boil, simmer for 10 minutes to get it to thicken. Drizzle syrup on both layers of the cake. To make the ganache—Place heavy cream and chocolate chips in a small pot. Simmer to melt, mix to blend. Spread ganache on both layers and place one layer on top of the other and the sides. Refrigerate until ready to serve. Serve chilled. This recipe yields about 10-12 servings.

FALL IN LOVE... SABARINA OR RUM BABA? — ISREAL ⭐ — SPECIALTY

For the dough—

3 eggs

2 sticks minus 2 tablespoons unsalted butter

1 1/4 cups warm milk

3 1/2 cups flour

1 tablespoon and 1 teaspoon dry yeast

3 tablespoons sugar

1 teaspoon vanilla extract

1/2 teaspoon salt

For the syrup—

4 cups of water

1/2 cup rum

3 cups sugar

For the cream—
8 ounces heavy cream
3 tablespoons sugar
1 tablespoon orange blossom water

Preheat the oven to 400F (200C). Place flour and yeast in a mixer, sugar and eggs, while the mixer is working on low speed add vanilla extract, slightly warm milk, melted butter, dough should be very sticky and soft. Cover the dough and let rise until it doubles in size. Spray cupcake baking pan with nonstick oil, punch dough to get some of the air out. Place a clear plastic sleeve inside a glass cup and fill up with dough batter, now fill up each cavity in the baking pan with the batter, bake for 20-25 minutes. Make the syrup—Place water in a small pot, add rum and sugar and bring it to a boil. Simmer for 10 minutes. Transfer each Sabarina to the syrup and cook for 30 second on each side, no more, (otherwise they will become crumbs), take the Sabarina out and set on a tray to cool down. Make the cream—In a mixer place the heavy cream, sugar, and orange blossom, mix until the cream is stiff. Use a sharp knife to cut a slit in the upper 1/3 part of the Sabarina. Fill up another plastic sleeve with the cream, pipe cream into the slit that is lifted. Serve with a sliced strawberry, sprinkle powdered sugar, serve chilled, what a nice little treat. Some of my friends love the Sabarina absolutely soaked in syrup, cheers to you. This recipe yields about 15-20 Sabarina desserts depending on the size you choose.

MAMA'S CANDID ORANGE, A GREAT PASSOVER TREAT

8-10 oranges with thick skin
4.4 pounds sugar
juice of one lemon

This is a large batch; you can cut all quantities in half for a smaller batch. Zest all oranges and brush with a vegetable brush. Place oranges in a large pan filled with hot water, bring to a boil. Discard the water and replace it with fresh water. Refrigerate the pot with oranges and water overnight. Next day wash the oranges again, discard the water, and return oranges to a clean pot. Pour all sugar on the oranges and refrigerate again for another night. This process is very important because the oranges will release their juice at this point. Now you are ready to place the oranges on the stove, simmer, on low covered for 2-3 hours. During this low heat cooking the oranges and the sugar will release juice and caramel that will blend and cook the oranges while a beautiful citrus aroma will spread in your kitchen. The pot should be covered the whole time, occasionally, flip the oranges to the other side. After the oranges release their juice and have cooked for 3 hours add the juice of one lemon and simmer for another 30 minutes. Serve as a sweet ending to a Passover meal, enrich the flavor of your charoset and serve on an ice cream.

MAMA'S EGGPLANT DREAM DESSERT — MOROCCO 🌺—IN MEMORY

2.2 pounds small eggplants 2-3" long (sometimes called Indian eggplants)
2.2 pounds sugar
2-3 cinnamon sticks
1 teaspoon ground cinnamon
1 teaspoon ground cloves
1 teaspoon ground ginger.
1 cup freshly squeezed lemon juice

Discard the leaves around the small eggplant but keep the stem intact. Use a fork to punch holes all over the eggplant, about 15 holes in each eggplant. Place a large pot on the stove, fill up with water and bring to a boil. Add the eggplants and boil for 5-7 minutes. Transfer to a colander and let cool a little. While the eggplants are cooling place a large pot with all other ingredients on the stove and simmer. When all the sugar and spices have melted insert the eggplants, one by one to the pot with the syrup. Do not use a spatula to mix, gently tilt from one side to another to mix. Cover the eggplant with the syrup. Cover the pot and simmer for about 2 hours. The eggplant should absorb most of the syrup by the end of the cooking. Transfer to a glass jar or container and top with all the extra syrup. This is a great dessert for Passover, cookie filling, roulade filling and my surprise—on ice cream!

MOFLETA — THE PASSOVER TREAT THAT IS MISSED ALL YEAR LONG — MOROCCO 🌺—IN MEMORY

For the dough—
2.2 pounds flour
1 1/4 teaspoon dry yeast
3 cups slightly warm water
1/4 cup vegetable oil
1 teaspoon salt

For serving—
honey and butter

This is a large quantity, this recipe will get about 35-40 servings, you can divide it to make only a half for a smaller group. Place all ingredients in a mixer, mix for 10 minutes. The more you mix the better the gluten will develop in this recipe which is very important. When making the whole amount, divide the dough into 35-40 small balls, place on an oily surface, cover entire batch with towel and let rise for one hour. Take a large pan and brush it with oil. Take one dough ball, drizzle oil on it, use your fingers to stretch it and make a circle the size of 7"- 8". Your hands should be very oily because this is a sticky dough. The oil helps with stretching the dough. When you have the first circle ready, place it in the pan, cook for 2-3 minutes, flip to the other side, dough should be cooked with some golden spots on it, that is normal. Get ready with the second circle of Mofleta, place it on the first one, flip to cook the outer side. Now you are ready to add another Mofleta, flip to cook the third one and so on. When you have about 10 cooked Mofleta, serve it right away, it should be hot from the pan when serving. Start a second batch. Guests apply honey and butter; they should say the Shehecheyanu and taste the very first flour product after Passover. This is a simple way to start eating flour again after Passover is over, and a delicious way the Moroccan Jewish community chose to celebrate the ending of Passover during the minimum party.

NO CHURN! BUT STILL THE BEST — CHOCOLATE HAZELNUTS ICE CREAM ⭐—SPECIALTY

1 1/4 cups very cold heavy cream
2/3 cup sweetened condensed milk
2 tablespoons chocolate liqueur
1/4 cup shaved chocolate or small chocolate chips
1/2 cup chopped hazelnuts

Place heavy cream, condensed milk, and chocolate liqueur in a mixer, mix slowly for 2 minutes, just to blend, then mix on high speed for another 5-7 minutes until cream gets thick, fold in the shaved chocolate or small chocolate chips and Hazelnuts, mix well. Transfer to a glass dish, level to get a smooth surface. Wrap twice with clear plastic. Place in a freezer for 4 hours but preferably overnight. This recipe yields about 8-10 servings.

POACHED PEAR IN RED WINE CHOCOLATE ⭐—SPECIALTY

For the pears—
1 bottle of sweet wine
8 large pears
1/2 cup sugar
1/2 teaspoon cinnamon

For the wine chocolate sauce—
4 ounces dark chocolate
2 tablespoons brandy or wine
4 tablespoons walnut oil
2 tablespoons honey
4 tablespoons water

This is a large amount; you can easily cut all quantities in half to serve it to a smaller group. Place pears, sugar, cinnamon, and wine in a pot, bring to a boil, reduce to simmer, cover, cook for 20 minutes. Transfer the pears to a plate to cool a little. In a small saucepan add all chocolate sauce ingredients, stir, bring to a boil and reduce immediately. Cover and simmer for 10-15 minutes until sauce is getting thick, it might need a little more time, so add another 5 minutes. When the sauce is simmering, slice the pears to 5-6 slices, no more, do it gently to keep the pear stem and ends intact, then open to spread the pear slices in a half circle shape. When the sauce is ready to drizzle, put a few drops on each plate around the pear and serve. This beautiful dessert can be served warm but most likely served cold and will yield about 8 servings unless if you cut the pears in half, then you can serve up to 16 servings.

POUCHED PEAR WRAPPED IN PASTRY, IN PORT WINE SAUCE 🏅 —AWARD WINNING

2 cups tap water
2 cups orange juice
2 cups port wine
1/2 cup sugar
1 tablespoon sugar
2 cinnamon sticks
6 whole cloves
3 black peppercorns
1 teaspoon orange or lemon zest
3 pears, preferably Bosch pears
2 cups flour
1-2 teaspoons salt
8 tablespoons unsalted butter (1/2 cup)
1 egg for dough
1 egg for brushing

1-2 tablespoons cold water

Preheat oven to 375F (190C). Place 2 cups port wine in a small pot, add 2 cups tap water, 2 cups orange juice, and 1/2 cup sugar, and mix. Bring to a boil, reduce, cook covered 30 minutes. Peel off the pears, keep the stems intact. Remove sauce from heat, add pears to pot, add 2 cinnamon sticks, 6 whole cloves, 3 black peppercorns, 1 teaspoon orange zest, return sauce to the heat, cook 2 hours on low heat, remove pears from sauce, let cool down. Return sauce to the heat and simmer to get a thicker sauce for the final step. Dry pears with a paper towel. Add 1 tablespoon sugar to a mixer, 2 cups flour, 1/4 teaspoon salt, 8 table-spoons unsalted butter, 1 egg, mix well, you can add 1-2 tablespoons of ice water if needed. Dough should be crumbs, that's normal. Wrap with clear plastic and refrigerate for 2 hours. Roll out the dough to open, dough should be 1/4". Use a pizza slicer to slice strips, about 1/2" wide. Wrap dough strip on the pear while gradually going up to cover the whole pear. When you wrapped a whole strip of dough take another strip, pinch to connect it to the first strip and keep circling the pear until all the pear is nicely wrapped with dough. You can also add a little piece of dough as a leaf and place it right by the stem. Brush the pastry pear with egg and bake for about 40 minutes until the pears turn golden brown. When ready to serve, drizzle wine sauce on the baked pears, serve chilled. This recipe yields 6 servings, half pear each serving.

PUMPKIN JAM — MAAJUN SLAVIA MOROCCAN ANGEL HAIR

2 pounds fresh pumpkin
2 pounds sugar
Juice of 2 lemons

Peel off pumpkin, place in hot water. Cover and cook for 25 minutes. Discard the water, let it cool. Shred the pumpkin by hand or use a food processor. Place in a clean pot, add all the sugar and simmer covered for 3-4 hours. Mix occasionally. Add the lemon juice and mix. Cook another 25-30 minutes. Let cool completely and transfer to a glass container. This jam is great on a labane cheese (see recipe in This and That category) and toast, great on ice cream, as a cookie filling and my surprise—great on brisket!

RICOTTA SQUARES DESSERT, QUICK, EASY & FLOUR LESS — ISRAEL ⏰—QUICK & EASY

3 cups ricotta cheese
2/3 cup raisins
2 tablespoons rum
1 teaspoon vanilla extract
1 teaspoon rose water—optional but recommended
1/4 cup corn starch
3 eggs
1 teaspoon lemon zest
1 cup sugar

Preheat the oven to 340F (170C). Place raisins in a small bowl, add the rum, toss to blend, soak for one hour. Add 3 eggs to a mixer mix for 3 minutes, add cornstarch, sugar, ricotta cheese, vanilla extract, and rose water if using and 1 teaspoon lemon zest. Mix at a slow speed to blend, then fold in the raisins with the rum. Transfer to a baking pan, level to get a smooth top surface. Bake for 18 minutes. Let cool down completely and refrigerate. Serve chilled. This recipe yields about 12-15 ricotta squares depending on their size.

YAFFA'S 2 MINUTES, 2 INGREDIENTS HAMANTASCHEN ⭐— SPECIALTY

1 package puff pastry, thawed
Jam—any kind

I call this the lazy day Hamantaschen. Preheat oven to 375F (190C). Open the puff pastry using a rolling pin to roll open the dough, use a glass to mark the circles on the dough. Add 1 teaspoon jam to each circle, fold 3 corners on the circle and pinch more to glue the sides to create a triangle. The jam filling should show a little bit, careful not to leave the triangle too open, it opens more during the baking. Brush with egg if desired and bake for 25-30 minutes until golden brown. Serve warm and crispy, this recipe yields about 24 servings.

YAFFA'S APPLE NUTS BAKLAVA

1 package of filo dough

Small bowl with vegetable oil or 4 sticks of unsalted melted butter
For the apples filling—
8 medium apples, cored, skin peeled off, thinly sliced
1 cup walnuts coarsely chopped
1 cup brown sugar
1 teaspoon cinnamon
3 tablespoons unsalted butter
zest of 1 orange
1/4 cup whiskey, rum or cognac.

For the syrup—
2/3 cup water
1/3 cup sugar
1 teaspoon cinnamon
1 teaspoon orange blossom

Heat the oven to 375F (190C). Place the apples in a pan with butter and sugar. Mix the butter and caramelize the sugar and nuts, cook apples for 5-7 minutes, add orange zest and alcohol, cook another 2-3 minutes for the alcohol to evaporate. Set aside. Open the filo package, if the filo is dry, cover with a kitchen towel and sprinkle with a few drops of water, if the filo is too wet do not cover at all. Place one filo dough on a large rectangle baking tray, brush with a little oil. Repeat with 6 more filo dough. Transfer the apples mixture to the baking pan, set them evenly on the filo dough. Add another filo dough to top the apples mixture, and brush with oil. Repeat with all the rest of the filo dough in the package, brush the top filo dough generously. Use a sharp knife to slice the filo dough to squares or diamonds. Transfer the baklava to the oven and bake for about 50 minutes until it puffs a little and turns golden brown. While the baklava is in the oven, make the syrup—Place syrup ingredients in a small pot, bring to a boil, reduce and simmer for 10 minutes. Drizzle the syrup on the baked baklava, especially between the cracks of each piece. This recipe yields about 34-36 servings.

YAFFA'S BOBKA WITH A SEPHARDIC TWIST ⭐—SPECIALTY

For the dough—
4 cups flour
1 tablespoon dry yeast
4 eggs
1/2 teaspoon salt
2 sticks unsalted butter (226grams), cubed
1/3 cup sugar
3/4 cup slightly warm water

For the filling—
1 cup cinnamon
1 cup sugar
2 sticks of unsalted butter

For the syrup—
1 cup water
1/2 cup sugar
1 teaspoon orange zest
1 tablespoon orange blossom

Preheat oven to 300F (148C). Making the filling—Add filling ingredients to mixer, mix to blend, 5-8 minutes, freeze for 2 hours. Add water, yeast and sugar, let sit 3-5 minutes. Add the eggs, butter, flour, mix 3-4 minutes, add salt. Knead dough for 8-10 minutes. Wrap the dough with clear plastic and refrigerate 4 hours or overnight. Make syrup—In a small pot place sugar and water, orange zest, bring to a boil, reduce and simmer for 10 minutes, remove from the heat, add 1 tablespoon orange blossom, set aside. When the dough is chilled knead it with your hands for a few minutes, divide the dough to 4 equal batches to get 4 Babkas. Flour the work surface, stretch to open the dough, use a rolling pin to create a long rectangle, use a spoon to scrape cinnamon filling and spread it on the dough, the filling should be very cold. Create a cinnamon line in the center of the dough, the size of 2" x 8". Fold in one side of the dough to cover the cinnamon filling, then place the other side of the dough on top of it. Use a rolling pin to stretch the dough and fold the whole dough to a double layer, stretch the dough again, fold the third time and stretch again. This will create those beautiful lines in the Bobka. After folding and stretching 4 times slice the dough into 3 long slices and braid the 3 strips like a simple challah. Brush with egg for color. Cover the Bobka with a kitchen towel and let rise for 30 minutes. Bake for 45-50 minutes. While the Bobka is still hot, brush with the syrup and drizzle more on top. Serve at room temperature or chilled. This recipe yields 4 Bobka cakes.

YAFFA'S CHAROSET FOR PASSOVER — MOROCCO ⭐— SPECIALTY

1/2 cup dates, pitted
1/4 cup raisins, seedless
1/2 cup prunes, pitted
1/4 cup almonds
1/4 cup walnuts
1 tablespoon rose water
1 cup sweet red wine
1/2 teaspoon cinnamon
1/4 teaspoon nutmeg
1/4 teaspoon cardamom
1/4 teaspoon ginger
1/4 teaspoon ground cloves

1/4 of the Moroccan candied orange, chopped (see recipe in Desserts)
Optional—a few dry or fresh rose petals for decoration

Place all ingredients except the candied orange in a bowl, mix well with the wine to soften the dry fruits. Transfer to a food processor, pulse for 4-5 times, use a spatula to mix and now let the mixer work again, mix for 2-3 minutes. Transfer to a serving plate and decorate with the chopped candied orange. If you can find rose petals decorate the plate with a few rose petals as well. If you are making the charoset just a few days before Passover, I suggest adding it to the serving plate where it will be served at the Seder table. If the Charoset was not totally devoured during Passover you can use it as a cookie filling, roulade filling, or check out the next cookie recipe for heavenly tasting chocolate covered cookies in the Cookies category.

YAFFA'S CHEESECAKE SOUFFLÉ ⭐—SPECIALTY

For the basic dough—
3/4 stick unsalted butter
1/4 cup sugar
1 teaspoon vanilla extract
2/3 cup flour

For the filling—
2 cups Philadelphia cream cheese
2 cups sour cream
1 cup sugar
1 teaspoon vanilla extract
1 teaspoon lemon zest
Pinch of salt
7 eggs, separated
4-5 tablespoons flour

1/4 cup corn starch

1 package instant vanilla pudding

1 cup milk

Preheat oven to 425F (218C). Place all dough ingredients in a mixer, mix on low to get a soft dough. If needed add 1-2 tablespoons of ice water. Remove dough from the mixer, knead by hand for a few minutes, wrap dough with clear plastic, refrigerate for 25 minutes. Line a baking pan with parchment paper, use your fingers to spread the dough all over the baking pan. Bake for 15 minutes. Set it aside. Place the sour cream, cream cheese, sugar, lemon zest, and salt in a mixer, mix to blend well, add the egg yolks, mix well. Add milk, corn starch, flour, instant vanilla pudding, mix well, set aside. In a clean mixer place egg white and mix to a stiff whip. Add 1/3 of the stiff whipped eggs to the egg yolks mixture, gently fold in to blend. Now add the rest of the whipped egg whites to the egg yolks mixture and carefully blend in to reserve as many air pockets as possible. Insert parchment paper along the inside of the baking pan to help the cake rise more if possible. Pour the batter in the baking pan one cup at a time, bake at 425F (218C) for 10 minutes then reduce the heat to 335F (168C) for 1 1/4 hours. Serve warm or chilled. This recipe yields about 10 servings.

YAFFA'S CLASSIC BAKLAVA ⭐—SPECIALTY

1 package of filo dough, thawed but cold

1 cup sugar

2 teaspoons cinnamon

1/2 teaspoon ground cloves

1 teaspoon cardamom

4 cups walnuts coarsely chopped

1 cup almonds coarsely chopped

2 cups vegetable oil or 4 sticks of unsalted butter, melted

For the syrup—

2/3 cup water

1/3 cup sugar

1 teaspoon cinnamon

1 tablespoon orange blossom

1 teaspoon lemon juice

Preheat oven to 375F (190C). Make the nuts filling—In a food processor place all nuts filling ingredients and pulse several times just enough to coarsely chop the nuts, transfer to a bowl. Open the filo package, check the filo dough in the package, if it looks dry and starts to chip sprinkle a few drops of water and cover with a towel, if the filo dough looks more wet than dry remove the towel. Transfer one filo to a rectangle baking pan, brush with the oil or butter, repeat with 6 more filo dough layer, add the nuts mixture, level the nuts layer, add all the filo layers while brushing each one with the oil or butter, this is what gets the dough to be so crispy. When all the filo is brushed with oil and one on top of the other use a sharp knife to cut the filo dough either to squares or diamonds. You should have about 36 pieces of Baklava. Transfer to the oven, bake for about 30-45 minutes until golden brown. Take out of the oven and drizzle all the syrup between the cracks of the squares. Let cool, serve cold or warm. This recipe yields about 34-36 pieces of baklava.

YAFFA'S EASY MALABI DESSERT PUDDING ⭐—SPECIALTY

3 tablespoons cornstarch

1/3 cup water

1 tablespoon rose water

2 cans of coconut milk (not coconut cream)

1/4 cup peeled pistachios, coarsely chopped

1/3 cup sugar

1 package unflavored gelatin

For the strawberries topping—

1 teaspoon rose water

1/3 cup sugar

3 cups fresh strawberries

Place the water, gelatin powder, and corn starch in a bowl, mix well to avoid any lumps, add coconut milk, cook on medium while mixing constantly with a whisk. Add the sugar, the cream will start getting thick, add the rose water, mix one more minute and remove from heat. Transfer the thick mixture to a glass dish, let it cool down to room temperature then refrigerate for 6 hours or overnight. While the malabi is being chilled make the strawberries topping. Remove the stems, cut each strawberry into 4 parts, set aside. Transfer the fresh strawberries to a small pot, add sugar and cook on low to melt the sugar. Add the rose water, cook 2 more minutes and remove from heat. Let the pot cool down to room temperature then refrigerate to be very cold. To serve, place some of the coconut malabi in a serving cup or small glass bowl, add strawberry topping on top, drizzle some of the pistachios on top and serve chilled. This recipe yields about 10 servings depending on the size of the serving.

YAFFA'S FLOUR-LESS & DAIRY FREE VANILLA PUDDING ROULADE FOR PASSOVER ⭐—SPECIALTY

For the GF dough—
2 tablespoons vegetable oil
3 tablespoons instant vanilla pudding
1/3 cup tapioca, quinoa, corn starch flour, or any other GF flour mixture
1/3 cup sugar
4 eggs

For the filling cream—
3 tablespoons vanilla pudding
1 tablespoon vegetable oil
3 tablespoons coconut milk
8 ounces heavy cream made of coconut, rich kosher, or any plant based heavy cream

For decoration—
1/4 cup dark chocolate chips

Preheat the oven to 340F (170C). In a mixer place eggs, mix for 1 minute, add sugar and mix 5 minutes on high speed to get a light, airy batter. Now slow the mixer's speed and gradually add 2 tablespoons vegetable oil. Add 1/3 cup corn starch or the GF flour of your choice, add vanilla pudding and mix the mixer on low speed to blend. Brush or spray a parchment paper and line a baking pan. Add the mixer's content to the baking pan and evenly spread. Bake in the oven for 20 minutes, cool down for 5 minutes. Roll the baked cake together with the parchment paper, do it gently, careful not to break the roulade, place with the seam facing down to secure. The roulade gets its shape from cooling down while it's rolled so this step is very important. While the roulade is cooling make the cream—Open the can of coconut milk and mix the milk with its liquid to blend in. Add 3 tablespoons of the coconut milk to the mixer, add 1 cup heavy cream, 3 tablespoons vanilla pudding, increase the mixer's speed, whip until you get a nice stiff cream. Gently and carefully roll to open the roulade, first add the cream to the first fold, then add the rest of the cream on all the roulade, make sure that the seam is facing down. Refrigerate. Melt the chocolate and vegetable oil on low heat, just enough to melt the chocolate. Let cool for a few minutes. Sprinkle powdered sugar on the roulade and drizzle chocolate all over the roulade to decorate. Serve chilled. This recipe yields one roulade with about 8-10 servings.

YAFFA'S HEAVENLY TORTA CAPUCHINA IS GLUTEN FREE — ITALY ⭐—SPECIALTY

6 eggs
2/3 cup sugar
5.5-6 ounces dark chocolate
Instead of the dark chocolate -5.5oz cocoa powder mixed with 1 cup water & 1 Tbsp. vegetable oil
2 tablespoons brandy or rum

1 teaspoon instant coffee

For the cream—
3 ounces dark chocolate
1.5 ounces unsalted butter or vegetable oil
2 teaspoons instant coffee
3 eggs, separated
3 tablespoons sugar

Preheat the oven to 350F (180C). Separate the 6 eggs, add the 6 egg yolks to the mixer. Whip the 6 egg yolks with the sugar for about 7 minutes. Add to the egg yolks the brandy, instant coffee, and chocolate or cocoa powder mixture. Whip the egg yolks mixture again for another 3-4 minutes. The mixture will look very glossy and chocolaty. In a clean mixer add all 6 egg whites and whip to get a stiff whip. Gently transfer 1/3 of the whipped egg whites to the egg yolks mixture, fold to mix, try to reserve as many air pockets as you can. Add the rest of the whipped egg whites to the chocolate mixture, gently mix by folding, until blended in. Line a round baking dish with parchment paper, pour the batter into the baking pan, bake for about 30-40 minutes, let cool down. Get ready with the chocolate cream—In a saucepan add instant coffee, dark chocolate, and vegetable oil. Simmer on low to melt the chocolate. Mix to blend. Separate the 3 eggs. Mix the melted chocolate into the bowl with egg yolks, mix to blend. Whip the egg whites to stiff. To assemble the cream, add the whipped eggs to the chocolate mixture and gently fold in. When the cake cools down completely, cover with the chocolate cream. Serve cold. This recipe yields one 8-9" cake, about 10-12 servings.

YAFFA'S NO BAKING FLOWERLESS TRUFFLES ⭐—SPECIALTY

1 cup almonds
1 cup dry apricots
1 1/4 cups powdered sugar
1 teaspoon rose water or orange blossom
1 tablespoon water
small bowl of cocoa powder

Place the almonds in a food processor, grind, add apricots, grind, add rose water and water, and grind to get a paste. If the mixture is still dry add another 1-2 tablespoons water. Use an ice cream scoop to scoop out some of the filling, form a ball and place on a tray. Dip each ball in the cocoa powder and cover. Transfer to a cookie container. Optional—you can dip the truffles in melted chocolate. Refrigerate until served. This recipe yields about 15-18 truffles.

YAFFA'S NO NUTS BAKLAVA ⭐—SPECIALTY

1 package filo dough
Small bowl of vegetable oil or 4 sticks unsalted butter, melted

For the filling—
1 cup shredded coconut
1 cup chocolate chip
1 cup dry cranberries
zest of 1 orange
1/4 cup orange liquor such as grand marine

For the syrup—
2/3 cup water
1/3 cup sugar
1/4 cup the same orange liquor

Preheat oven to 375F (190C). Place all filling ingredients except the orange liquor in a mixer, mix to blend. Now add the liquor and mix well, set aside. Open the filo package, if the filo looks dry and starts to chip cover with wet towel and sprinkle with a few drops of water. If the filo looks sticky and wet do not cover it. Place one filo on a rectangle baking tray, brush with oil or butter. Transfer all the filling to the filo dough, level the filling to have a smooth surface. Place a filo dough on the filling, brush with oil, repeat with all the filo in the package. Use a sharp knife to slice the Baklava into squares or diamonds. Bake for about 50-60 minutes to get a puffy dough and golden brown. While the baklava is baking make the syrup—Place the water and sugar in a small pot and bring to a boil, reduce and cook for 10 minutes on simmer, add the orange liquor in the last 2 minutes. Drizzle the syrup in between the cracks of the slices. This recipe yields about 34-36 pieces.

YAFFA'S "NOT TO SKIP" NO CHURN ROSE WATER EASY ICE CREAM ⭐—SPECIALTY

1 1/4 cups very cold heavy cream
2/3 sweetened condensed milk
2 tablespoons rose water or orange blossom water
2 tablespoons orange liqueur
Optional—Yaffa's candied orange, 2 slices chopped

This heavenly tasting cce cream is 3 minutes work. Place all ingredients in a mixer, except the candied orange if using. Mix to blend until thick, about 5-7 minutes. If using the candied orange this is the step where you add it and gently blend with the cream. Pour the thick cream into a deep glass dish and wrap the dish with clear plastic, twice. Transfer to the freezer for 4 hours but preferably overnight. Serve frozen, this recipe yields about 6-8 servings.

YAFFA'S OWN, CHOCOLATE HAZELNUT BOBKA ⭐—SPECIALTY

For the dough—
4 cups flour
1 tablespoon dry yeast
4 eggs
1/2 teaspoon salt
2 sticks unsalted butter, cubed
1/3 cup sugar
3/4 cup warm water

For the chocolate hazelnut filling—
1 cup hazelnuts
1 cup sugar
2 sticks unsalted butter

zest of one orange
1 teaspoon orange blossom

For the syrup—
2/3 cup water
1/2 cup sugar
1 tablespoon orange blossom

Preheat oven to 300F (148C). Make the filling—Add filling ingredients to mixer, mix to blend, 5-8 minutes, freeze for 2 hours. Make the dough—Add water, yeast, and sugar to a bowl, combine, let sit for 3-5 minutes. Add the eggs, butter, and flour, mix for 3-4 minutes, add salt. Knead dough for 8-10 minutes. Wrap the dough with clear plastic and refrigerate 4 hours or overnight. Make the syrup—In a small pot place sugar and water, bring to a boil, reduce and simmer for 10 minutes, remove from the heat, add the 1 tablespoon orange blossom, set aside. When the dough is chilled knead it with your hands for a few minutes, divide the dough into 4 equal batches to get 4 Babkas. Flour the work surface, stretch to open the dough, use a rolling pin to create a long rectangle, use a spoon to scrape chocolate hazelnuts filling and spread it on the dough, the filling should be very cold. Create a chocolate line in the center of the dough, in the size of 2" x 8". Fold in one side of the dough to cover the filling, then place the other side of the dough on top of it. Use a rolling pin to stretch the dough and fold the whole dough to a double layer, stretch the dough again, fold the third time and stretch again. This will create those beautiful lines in the Bobka. After folding and stretching 4 times slice the dough into 3 long slices and braid the 3 strips like a simple challah. Brush with egg for color. Cover the Bobka with a kitchen towel and let rise for 30 minutes. Bake for 45-50 minutes. While the Bobka is still hot, brush with the syrup and drizzle more on top. Serve at room temperature or chilled. This recipe yields 4 Bobka cakes.

YAFFA'S PASSOVER CHOCOLATE & PEANUT BUTTER CUPCAKE IS FLOUR-LESS & QUICK ⭐—SPECIALTY

10.5 ounces chocolate chips (300 grams)

5 ounces unsalted butter (150 grams)

2/3 cup almond flour

1 tablespoon cornstarch or other GF flour

10 tablespoons peanut butter

3 eggs

3 egg yolks

3/4 cup sugar

Preheat the oven to 400F (200C). Place chocolate chips and butter in a double boiler if you have one or in a small pot, simmer on very low! Careful not to scorch the chocolate, it should be silky and soft, transfer to a small bowl. Let the chocolate cool down for 10 minutes. Add 3 eggs and 3 egg yolks to a mixer. Add 3/4 cup sugar and mix for 3 minutes. Reduce the speed, gradually add the chocolate mixture, add 2/3 cup almond flour, 1 tablespoon corn starch or any other gluten-free flour, mix to blend. Spray or oil a cupcake baking pan and add 3 tablespoons of the batter, add 1-2 teaspoons peanut butter, and top with another 1-2 tablespoons of the chocolate batter. Bake for 15-17 minutes only, let the cupcakes cool down. Serve at room temperature. Store in the refrigerator, this recipe yields about 12 cupcakes.

YAFFA'S SHAVUOT LIMONCELLO CAKE — ITALY ⏰—QUICK & EASY

5.29 ounces unsalted butter
1 1/4 cups sugar
juice of 1 lemon, discard the seeds
zest of one lemon
1/4 cup yogurt
1/4 cup limoncello liqueur
1 1/3 cup almond flour (or any other flour)
1 cup flour
1 teaspoon baking powder
4 large eggs

For the syrup—
3/4 cup sugar
1/2 cup lemon juice
1/4 cup limoncello liqueur

Preheat the oven to 335F (160C). Place unsalted butter, sugar, lemon zest, lemon juice, eggs, and yogurt in a mixer and mix for 3 minutes, add the limoncello. Add the almond flour (or the other flour), keep mixing. Now add the 1 cup flour and mix on a medium speed, add baking powder. Brush a 8-9" pan with oil or nonstick spray, transfer batter to baking pan and bake for 50 minutes. While the cake is in the oven make the limoncello syrup. Place all syrup ingredients (except limoncello) in a small pot, bring to a boil, remove from the heat, add the limoncello liqueur to the syrup. When the cake is ready, drizzle the syrup on it and let cool down. This cake yields 10-12 servings.

YAFFA'S SIGNATURE APPLE STRUDEL ⭐—SPECIALTY

1 package filo dough
small bowl filled with vegetable oil or melted butter
5 medium apples, skin peeled off, thinly sliced, sprinkled with some lemon juice
1 teaspoon lemon zest
1/2 teaspoon cinnamon
2 tablespoons cognac or amaretto or whiskey
1/4 cup sugar
1/4 cup raisins
1/4 cup walnuts
1 egg for brushing

Preheat oven to 350F (180C). Add about 2 tablespoons vegetable oil to a pan, add apples, raisins, alcohol, sugar, cinnamon, walnuts, and lemon zest, bring to a boil, reduce to simmer until all alcohol evaporates and the sauce thickens around the apples a little. Cook for about 8 minutes. Transfer to a bowl and cool down. Open the filo dough, and take out one filo dough, place on a baking pan, brush with a little oil immediately, if the filo dough feels dry sprinkle a few drops of water and cover it with a kitchen towel. Repeat with 6 filo dough layers and brush with oil. Check to see that the apples are cold, transfer apples to the filo dough and arrange them in one line on the wide side of the filo dough, fold in the two sides to secure from leaking and start rolling the filo dough like a roulade, make sure that the seam is facing down. Brush the top side with egg and transfer to the oven. Bake for 35-45 minutes until golden brown. This recipe yields about 8-10 servings.

YAFFA'S SIMPLE FRENCH APPLE PIE IN A PAN TART TATTIN — FRANCE ⏰—QUICK & EASY

5 apples, medium size, peeled, cored, thick sliced
2/3 cup sugar
1 teaspoon cinnamon
2 tablespoons unsalted butter
1 sheet of puff pastry

Preheat the oven to 350F (180C). Soak the apples slices in a bowl with cold water and 1 tablespoon lemon juice until you are done slicing all apples. Use a large pan to fit all apples in a single layer, add the butter and brush all the pan with it, now add the apples, arrange them in a circle shape and cover the whole base of the pan. Sprinkle the sugar on the apples and simmer to cook until all sugar melts and infuses with the apples and butter. Cook for about 7-10 minutes to caramelize the apples. Set it aside. Use a rolling pin to open the puff pastry dough and create a circle, about the same size as the pan you are using. Transfer the dough circle to the pan and cover the apples. Tuck the extra dough into the pan to cover all the apples. Brush with an egg, transfer to the oven and bake until the top is golden brown, about 20-25 minutes. Get a serving cake tray ready, place it on the pan, use both hands to flip the pan upside down so that the apples show on the top surface. Serve warm or cold. This recipe yields about 12 servings.

YAFFA'S SOOOO EASY HANUKKAH SUFGANIYOT FILLED WITH CREAM PATISIER ⭐—SPECIALTY

For the dough—

1.5 cup water

5 cups flour

1 tablespoon dry yeast

1/2 cup vegetable oil

3 eggs

1 1/3 cup sugar

hint of salt

For the cream patisserie—

1 sleeve vanilla bean

1 cup milk

1 cup sugar

3 egg yolks

2 1/2 tablespoons corn starch

2 1/4 tablespoons unsalted butter

Make the cream patisserie—Use a sharp knife to split the vanilla bean sleeve, scrape the inside contents, set aside. In a small pot add milk, egg yolks, sugar, and vanilla bean contents. Heat over medium heat while mixing constantly. When the mixture starts boiling remove from the heat, add unsalted butter while mixing all the time. Transfer to a bowl, cover with clear plastic, refrigerate for a minimum of 3 hours. Make the dough—Place the slightly warm water and yeast in a mixer, mix, let sit for 3-5 minutes. Add the other dough ingredients and mix for 10 minutes. The dough should be very sticky, but it is normal. Sprinkle flour in a bowl, transfer the dough to the bowl, sprinkle more flour on top. Cover with clear plastic and let rise until double in size. Remove dough from the bowl, flour the surface of a work area, knead the dough for a few minutes. Divide the dough into 2 batches, cover one batch and work with the other batch. Roll dough open to a flat surface 1/4" thick, use glass in the dough to get circles, place all dough circles in a floured baking pan. Cover and let rise at least for one hour. Repeat with the second batch of dough. Add vegetable oil to a small pot, oil should be deep, about half of the height of the pot. Place one circle of dough in the pot, cover, cook for 1-2 minutes, uncover and flip and cover the Sufganiya to cook on the other side, until it turns golden and puffy. Remove and add 2-3 circles of dough, repeat the process. Fill up a sleeve of cream with the cream patisserie, push to insert the cream into the Sufganiya. Sprinkle with powdered sugar, serve warm, Sufganiya can be reheated in oven for 5 minutes. This recipe yields about 12-15 Sufganeyot, depending on their size.

YAFFA'S SWEET POTATO JAM — THE MOROCCAN ANGEL HAIR ⭐—SPECIALTY

2 pounds sweet potato

2 pounds sugar
juice of 2 lemons

Peel sweet potatoes and place in hot water. Cover and cook for 25 minutes. Discard the water, let cool. Shred the sweet potatoes by hand or use a food processor. Place in a clean pot, add all the sugar and simmer covered for 3-4 hours. Mix occasionally. Add the lemon juice and mix. Cook another 25-30 minutes. Let cool completely and transfer to a glass container. This jam is great on a labane (see recipe in This and That category) cheese/toast, great on ice cream, and my surprise—great on brisket!

YAFFA'S SWEET POTATO JAM ROULADE

6 cups flour (for 4 roulade)
1 cup water
1 tablespoon baking powder
1 egg for brushing

For the filling—
1/2 cup of Yaffa's sweet potatoes jam for each roulade (see recipe in This and That category)
2 cups vegetable oil

Preheat oven to 340F (170C). Place all the dough ingredients in a mixer, mix for 8-10 minutes. No need to let the dough rise. Divide dough to 4 batches, use a rolling pin to open the dough of one batch to a large rectangle, dough should be less than 1/4" thick. Transfer 1/2 cup of the jam onto the dough, spread evenly all over the dough. Start rolling the dough from one side and keep rolling into a roulade until all dough is rolled in. Brush the top side of the roulade with egg and make sharp slits for decoration on the top side, about 3-4 slits. Repeat with the other 3 batches to get 4 small roulades. Bake for 30 minutes, let cool. Store in an airtight container. This recipe yields the total of 16-20 servings.

YAFFA'S THANKSGIVING MINI PUMPKIN CREAM CHEESE BITES ⭐—SPECIALTY

For the batter—
1 cup vegetable oil
1 1/2 cups brown sugar
3 large eggs
1 cup pumpkin purée
1/2 teaspoon baking soda
1/2 teaspoon baking powder
2 cups flour
3 teaspoons pumpkin spice mix (see recipe in This and That category)
1/2 cup Never stick formula (see recipe in This and That category)

For the filling—
1 cup cream cheese
1 cup powdered sugar
pinch of salt
1 teaspoon vanilla extract

Preheat oven to 350F (180C). Place vegetable oil in the mixer, add brown sugar, 3 eggs, increase the speed and mix for 2-3 minutes. Add pumpkin purée, baking powder, baking soda, mix well for 1 minute. Add pumpkin spice mix (see recipe), add flour, mix well, about 4 minutes, add salt. In a separate bowl add cream cheese, powder sugar, vanilla extract, butter, and salt, mix to get a creamy silky filling. Spray a cupcake baking sheet with nonstick spray, or brush generously with my winning formula for Never stick formula recipe (see recipe). Add only

1 tablespoon of batter to each cake-let cup, add 1 tablespoon cream cheese filling to each, and top off with 1 more tablespoon of the pumpkin batter. Do the same if you would like one big cake instead of cupcakes. Transfer cupcake baking sheet to the oven. Bake for 25 minutes, let cool, refrigerate. This recipe is one cake-let per a serving, so it all depends how many cake-lets you make. If you are making one large cake, bake for 45-50 minutes at the same temperature.

YAFFA'S WOW! VANILLA PUDDING CHEESECAKE ⭐— SPECIALTY

2 cups flour
2 teaspoons baking powder
1/3 cup sugar
1 teaspoon vanilla extract
1 1/2 sticks unsalted butter, cubed (6 oz, 56 grams)
4 egg yolks

For the cheesecake filling—
16 ounces whip cream
1 cup sugar
1 package instant vanilla pudding
1 cup sour cream
3 cups Philadelphia cream cheese

Preheat the oven to 350F (180C). Place all dough ingredients in a food processor, pulse a few times to get a crumbled sticky dough. Divide the dough into 2 baking pans. In one baking pan place 3/4 of the dough, in the second baking pan place just a 1/4 of the dough. Use your finger to arrange the large batch of dough in the first baking pan, this will be the basic layer for the cake, and the small batch of dough will become the crumbs for the top level of the cheesecake. Bake for 20 minutes until golden and take out. Let the basic dough cool completely. Make the filling—Place all filling ingredients in a mixer and mix on medium speed until a thick cream, refrigerate. Make sure that the small batch of dough is cold, use your fingers or a potato masher to make coarse crumbs out of the dough, set aside. Transfer the filling to the large baking pan, layer the filling evenly and top with the crumbs. Tap the crumbs a little to get a stable layer on the filling and refrigerate for several hours or overnight to stabilize the pudding for easy slicing. Serve chilled from the refrigerator. This recipe yields about 10-12 servings.

COOKIES
& CANDY

HELPFUL HINTS

- Unbaked cookie dough can be covered and refrigerated for up to 24 hours or frozen in an airtight container for up to 9 months.
- Bake one cookie sheet at a time on the middle oven rack.
- Decorate cookies with chocolate by placing cookies on a rack over waxed paper. Dip the times of a fork into melted chocolate and wave the fork gently back and forth to make line decorations.
- Some cookies need indentations on top to fill with jam or chocolate. Use the rounded end of a honey dipper.
- Dip cookie cutters in flour or powdered sugar and shake off excess before cutting. For chocolate dough, dip cutters in baking cocoa.
- Tin coffee cans make excellent freezer containers for cookies.
- If you only have one cookie sheet on hand, line it with parchment paper. While one batch is baking, load a second sheet of parchment paper to have another batch ready to bake. Cleanup will be easier.

- When a recipe calls for packed brown sugar, fill the correct size measuring cup with sugar and use one cup size smaller to pack the brown sugar into its cup.
- Cut up dried fruit often sticks to the blade of your knife. To prevent this problem, coat the blade of your knife in a thin film of vegetable spray before cutting.
- Instead of folding nuts into brownie batter, sprinkle on top of batter before baking. This keeps nuts crunchy instead of soggy.
- Only use glass or shiny metal pans. Dark or nonstick pans will cause brownies to become soggy and low in volume.
- When making bars, line the pan with aluminum foil and prepare as directed. The bars can be lifted out, and cleanup is easy.
- Cutting bars is easier if you score the bars right as the pan leaves the oven. When the bars cool, cut along the scored lines.
- Use a double boiler for melting chocolate to prevent it from scorching. A slow cooker on the lowest setting also works well for melting chocolate, especially when coating a large amount of candy.
- Parchment paper provides an excellent nonstick surface for candy. Waxed paper should not be used for high-temperature candy.

ABADI COOKIES ARE A SAVORY DELIGHT FOR A LAZY DAY — ISRAEL ⭐—SPECIALTY

2 cups all-purpose flour
1 tablespoon sesame seeds
1 teaspoon salt
1/4 teaspoon black pepper
1/3 cup vegetable oil
1/2 cup club soda
Optional—mushroom soup powder, recommended
Optional brush with egg
Optional—1/2 teaspoon garlic powder
Other flavoring options—black pepper, anise seeds, za'atar

Preheat oven to 350F (180C). Add all ingredients to a mixer and knead for 5 minutes, if the dough is too dry add 1-2 tablespoons cold water. No need to let the dough rise. Take about 1/4 cup of dough, roll to a round ring or just simple 3" sticks and place on the baking tray. Brush with egg if using and bake for 20-25 minutes until golden brown. Let cool completely and store in an airtight container. This recipe yields about 25-30 cookies.

EASY PURIM HAMANTASCHEN #1 — ISRAEL ⏰—QUICK & EASY

For the dough—
2 sticks unsalted butter
1 cup sugar
3 eggs
zest from one orange
1/4 cup orange juice
2 teaspoons baking powder
4 2/3 cups flour

For the filling—
1/2 pound dry prunes, pitted
1 cup raisins/dates
1/2 cup apricot jam
2 tablespoons honey
1/2 cup walnuts—optional
1 teaspoon lemon zest

1 egg for brushing
powdered sugar to sprinkle

Preheat oven to 350F (180C). Place all filling ingredients in a food processor and grind to a coarse paste, set aside. Add flour, sugar, and baking powder to a mixer, mix for 2 minutes, add all other dough ingredients and mix for 8-10 minutes. Wrap dough with clear plastic, refrigerate for one hour. Use a rolling pin to open the dough, the dough should be about 1/4" thick. Use a cup to mark circles in the dough. Add 2 teaspoon of the sweet filling to each circle. Now pinch 3 sides/corners of the circle to get a triangle shape, make sure to pinch enough so that the circle does not open during the baking. Brush with the egg and bake for 20-25 minutes until golden brown. Let cool down completely, sprinkle with some powdered sugar, store in an airtight container.

JERUSALEM BISCOTOSH — ISRAEL 🌺—IN MEMORY

4 cups flour
1 tablespoon baking powder
1 tablespoon salt
2 eggs
1 tablespoon white vinegar
1/3 cup water
9 ounces salted butter, cold

For brushing—
1/3 cup mixed or just one of these seeds—sesame seeds, fennel seeds, cumin seeds, anise seeds, (chili flax-optional)

Preheat oven to 482F (250C). In a mixer bowl place flour, baking powder. and salt, mix to blend. Add eggs, vinegar, water, and butter, knead for 6-8 minutes on speed #1 on your mixer. Place one small bowl with egg and a second small bowl with all the seeds mixture. Divide the dough into small balls the size of a ping pong ball. Transfer to a baking pan lined with foil. Use your hand to flatten the dough ball and use a finger to poke and make a hole in the dough to get a doughnut shape. Make sure that the hole is large enough so that the baking process does not close it during the baking. Brush the cookie/donut with egg and sprinkle a few seeds, bake 12-15 minutes until golden. Let cool down completely, store in a tight box or in the refrigerator, this recipe yields about 30-35 cookies.

MAMA'S SFINGE — DOUGHNUTS 🌺—IN MEMORY

2.2 pounds all-purpose flour
2 ounces yeast
3.5-4 cups lukewarm water
1/2 teaspoon salt
Powdered sugar to sprinkle
Vegetable oil for frying

Place first 4 ingredients in a mixer, mix for 8-10 minutes. Transfer dough to a bowl and cover, let rise for 2 hours. Return to the mixer and knead for another 3 minutes. The dough should be very sticky, but it is normal. Heat the oil to a medium heat. Grab about 1/4 cup of dough, oil your hands and make a ring of dough with a large hole in the middle. Place doughnut in the hot oil and fry 1 minute on each side, remove to a colander to drain. Serve warm sprinkled with powdered sugar. This recipe yields about 30-35 doughnuts.

RIEFA — MAMA'S TEA COOKIES 🌺—IN MEMORY

2.2 pounds all-purpose flour

1 1/2 cups sugar

3 eggs

1/2 cup freshly squeezed orange juice

1 cup vegetable oil

1 tablespoon baking powder

1 tablespoon sesame seeds

1 tablespoon fennel seeds

Preheat the oven to 350F (180C). Place all dry ingredients in a mixer and mix for 2-3 minutes. Add all wet ingredients and knead for 7 minutes. Use a rolling pin to open the dough to a flat sheet, about 1/4" thick, use a cookie cutter, a cup, or do it in the traditional way by slicing them in uneven shapes. Poke the cookies with a fork, poke 10 times at least for each cookie. Bake for 20-30 minutes until golden color. Let cool completely, store in an airtight container, this aromatic cookie recipe yields about 15-20 large cookies.

YAFFA'S HAMANTASCHEN PURIM COOKIES, #2 — ISREAL 🥇 — AWARD WINNING

For the melt in your mouth dough—
2 egg yolks
2 sticks minus 2 tablespoons butter
2 cups flour
1 tablespoon sugar
pinch of salt
1 teaspoon vanilla
1 teaspoon orange zest
1/2 teaspoon baking powder

Options for the filling—combine 2 or more
jam
chocolate chips
date spread
Nutella
raisins
egg for brushing
powdered sugar to sprinkle

Preheat the oven to 350F (180C). Place all dry ingredients in a food processor, pulse twice just to mix. Add all wet ingredients, pulse just enough to get a crumbled dough, about 6-8 times. If dough does not come together, add 1-2 tablespoons cold water. Transfer dough to a surface and knead it with hands to help it bind enough to make a dough ball. Sprinkle some flour on your working surface, divide the dough into 2 balls. Refrigerate one half and start working with the other. Use a rolling pin to open the dough, the dough should be a little less than 1/4". Use a cup to cut circles in the dough, add about 2 teaspoons of the filling of your choice to the circle, pinch to close the 3 corners of the circle. Make sure that the triangle is tight and secured enough so that it does not open during baking. Brush with egg, bake for about 20-25 minutes until golden brown, let cool completely. Sprinkle powdered sugar. This recipe yields about 20-25 cookies.

YAFFA'S MUST HAVE PEANUT COOKIES FOR MIMUNA PARTY — MOROCCO

3 cups peanuts, not roasted, not salted
1 3/4 cups sugar
5 tablespoons flour
1 teaspoon baking powder
3 eggs
1/2 teaspoon cinnamon
1/2 teaspoon cloves
1 teaspoon vanilla extract
powdered sugar in a small bowl
1/2 teaspoon dry ginger

Preheat oven to 350F (180C). Place peanuts on a baking pan, transfer to an oven for 5-7 minutes to roast, let cool. Place peanuts between your hands and rub your hands together to remove the shell. Place peanuts in a food processor with the sugar and grind for 5 minutes, open and scrape the sides, close and grind again for another 3 minutes. Place peanuts in a bowl and add all other ingredients except the powdered sugar, mix to combine. Use an ice cream scoop to scoop out a small amount and roll it into a ball. Transfer to a small paper cup and place in a baking pan. Bake for 20 minutes, let cool completely. Roll each cookie ball in the powdered sugar bowl. Serve at room temperature. Store in a tight container, these cookies will last a long time. This recipe yields about 40 cookies.

HELPFUL HINTS

- Never overcook foods that are to be frozen. Foods will finish cooking when reheated. Don't refreeze cooked, thawed foods.
- When freezing foods, label each container with its contents and the date it was put in the freezer. Always use frozen, cooked foods within 1-2 months.
- To avoid teary eyes when cutting onions, cut them under cold running water, or briefly place them in the freezer before cutting.
- Fresh lemon juice will remove onion scent from hands.
- To get the most juice out of fresh lemons, bring them to room temperature and roll them under your palm against the kitchen counter before cutting and squeezing.
- Add raw rice to the salt shaker to keep the salt free flowing.
- Transfer jelly and salad dressings to small kitchen squeeze bottles—no more messy, sticky jars!
- Ice cubes will help sharpen garbage disposal blades.
- Separate stuck-together glasses by filling the inside glass with cold water and setting both glasses in hot water.

- Clean CorningWare® by filling it with water and dropping in two denture cleaning tablets. Let stand for 30-45 minutes.
- Always spray your grill with nonstick cooking spray before grilling to avoid sticking.
- To make a simple polish for copper bottom cookware, mix equal parts of flour and salt with vinegar to create a paste.
- Purchase a new coffee grinder and mark it "spices." It can be used to grind most spices; however, cinnamon bark, nutmeg, and others must be broken up a little first. Clean the grinder after each use.
- In a large shaker, combine 6 parts salt and 1 part pepper for easy seasoning.
- Save your store-bought bread bags and ties—they make the perfect storage bags for homemade bread.
- Next time you need a quick ice pack, grab a bag of frozen peas or other vegetables out of the freezer.

AVOCADO LEMON DIP ❤️—HEART HEALTHY

1 large avocado
1 tablespoon freshly squeezed lemon juice
1 tablespoon extra-virgin/cold press olive
1/2 teaspoon garlic powder
1/4-1/2 teaspoon salt
1/4 teaspoon black pepper oil

Use a fork to mash avocado in a bowl, add all other ingredients and mix well, taste to check flavor. Transfer to a glass container and cover. Refrigerate and serve cold. This recipe yields about 12-15 ounces lemon spread.

AWARD WINNING OLIVE TAPENADE 🥇—AWARD WINNING

1 full cup of green olives, pickled and pitted
1 tablespoon fresh orange zest
1/4 cup walnuts
1 tablespoon cognac (or rum, whiskey)
2 anchovies fillets
1/4 cup and 1 tablespoon freshly squeezed lemon juice
3 garlic cloves
1/4 cup extra virgin/cold press olive oil
1/4 teaspoon pepper (taste before adding)

Tapenade is a great top for toasts and crackers with cheese. Place all ingredients in a food processor except salt and pepper, mix on medium speed for 1 minute. Scrape all sides to help blend in and mix again on high speed for 2-3 minutes, taste to see if salty enough, remember that olives and anchovies are already salty. Add salt only if needed, add pepper. Mix for 1 more minute, tapenade should be smooth but a little grainy as well. This recipe yields about 12-14 ounces tapenade spread.

AWARD WINNING! SCRUMPTIOUS GARLIC SPREAD 🏅 —AWARD WINNING

1 cup fresh garlic clove, peeled, (as many peeled garlic cloves as you can fit in one cup before grinding)

2 tablespoons vegetable oil (no olive oil on this one)

1/4 cup and 1 teaspoon freshly squeezed lemon juice

1/4 teaspoon each salt and pepper

4 tablespoons mayonnaise

1-2 tablespoons of vegetable oil to top with

Place all ingredients in a food processor and mix on high speed for 3 minutes. Scrape sides of the mixer bowl to help garlic blend in. Turn on mixer again and mix on high speed for another 3-4 minutes. Transfer to a container and drizzle a thin layer of vegetable oil on top surface. Refrigerate, serve cold, this award-winning recipe yields about 12-15oz. garlic spread.

BAHARAT SPICE MIX ⭐—SPECIALTY

1 teaspoon black pepper
1 teaspoon coriander seeds
1 small cinnamon stick
1 teaspoon whole cloves
1/2 teaspoon allspice
2 teaspoons cumin
1 teaspoon cardamon pods
1/2 teaspoon nutmeg, grated

Place all spices in a spice grinder and grind for 3-5 minutes to get the consistency of powder, transfer to a small glass jar, store in a cool dark place. Use to flavor dishes and soups, this amount is enough for several uses, Baharat is a very dominant spice mix, use only the amount that the recipe calls for which is usually 1-2 teaspoons.

BERBER SPICE MIX 🌺—IN MEMORY

1/4 cup ground sweet paprika
1 teaspoon hot paprika
1 teaspoon coriander seeds, finely ground
1 teaspoon cumin seeds, finely ground
1 teaspoon salt
1 teaspoon black pepper, finely ground
1/2 teaspoon ground white pepper
1/2 teaspoon English pepper
1/2 teaspoon ground nutmeg
1/2 teaspoon ground mace

1 1/2 teaspoons dry ginger, ground

1/2 teaspoon ground cinnamon

1/2 teaspoon turmeric powder

1/2 teaspoon saffron threads

This spice mix is known more in use by the Sahara Desert people. It has a lot of similarities to the famous Ras Al Hanut but different in some spices and quantities. Mix all spices and transfer to a jar, preferably a glass jar. Store in a cool dark place away from the sun, this spice mix amount is large, use only as much as the recipe calls for which is usually, 1-2 teaspoons.

CLASSIC RAS AL HANUT SPICE MIX — MOROCCO ⭐— SPECIALTY

1 tablespoon nutmeg

1 tablespoon sweet paprika

1 tablespoon black pepper

1 tablespoon ginger

1 tablespoon turmeric

1 tablespoon cardamon

1 tablespoon cinnamon

1 tablespoon mace

This is the famous Moroccan mix that every lady of the house creates for her own cooking and has a pride in her own combination. The spices mentioned here are very basic and can grow to be up to 35 different spices. Use a dry pan to toast all the ingredients over low heat until fragrant, grind in a spice grinder and transfer to a glass jar. Store in a dark cool area. This spice mix amount is large, use only as much as the recipe calls for which is usually, 1-2 teaspoons.

DELIGHTFUL RED BELL PEPPER HARISSA — MOROCCO

2.2 pounds fresh red bell peppers, cubed, seeds and stems removed
5-6 small garlic cloves, skin peeled
1 tablespoon ground cumin
1/2 cup vegetable or light olive oil
1 tablespoon sweet or hot paprika
2 tablespoons tomato paste
1 tablespoon salt
1/2 cup white vinegar

Start by placing red bell peppers and garlic in a food processor, grind for 2 minutes. Add all other ingredients and grind for 3-4 minutes, open the food processor and scrape the side of bowl to help blend all ingredients, grind another 2-3 minutes. Transfer to a container and refrigerate. This Harissa is great to flavor eggplants and other roasted or fried vegetables and is delicious as a spread in every sandwich. This recipe is about the amount of 16-20 ounces jar.

EASY BUT DIVINE, MOROCCAN PRESERVED LEMONS, THE NEVER-ENDING GIFT ⏰—QUICK & EASY

3 fresh lemons with thick peels
3 tablespoons salt
enough lemon juice to cover a medium glass jar
olive oil to top the jar

Brush lemons with a vegetable brush and dry well. Slice lemons in half but keep the ends intact, slice the halves again to get 4 quarters of lemons but do not cut the quarters all the way, make sure that the base of the lemon is still together, and all quarters are still intact. Add 1 tablespoon of salt and pour it in between the 4 quarters, place the lemon in a sterilized glass jar, repeat with all lemons and salt. Cover the lemons with enough lemon juice to top the lemons, drizzle about 2-3 tablespoons cold press olive oil on top. Close the jar tight and place in a sunny, lighted area for the first week, then transfer to a room temperature area for another 10 days. Remember to add a new lemon with salt whenever you use a whole lemon, this will make sure that you will never be out of these delicious, preserved lemons, usually I add 1/2 lemon sliced to one recipe of tagine and 1/4 lemon sliced to a salad, the rest remains in the jar and replace with fresh lemons, oil and salt when the jar is almost empty.

FISH DIP FOR EVERY FISH DISH & DRESSING NOT TO SKIP ⏰— QUICK & EASY

0.7 ounce butter
2-3 large garlic cloves, peeled and minced
2 shallot onions thinly chopped
1/4-1/2 teaspoon each salt and white pepper
1 tablespoon fresh parsley, chopped, leaves only
1/2 cup dry white wine

Place butter, shallots, and garlic in a frying pan, cook on low heat while mixing constantly, do not let the butter burn or turn brown. Add desired salt and white pepper, add parsley and mix. Gradually add white wine and mix for 1 minute. Serve with grilled fish of any kind. Refrigerate extra sauce. The recipe yields enough dressing for one large fish.

FOR ALL OF YOU LOVERS OF HOT SPICY, BUT FLAVORFUL — SCHUG — YEMEN 🌶—HOT & SPICY

4 hot green peppers such as Anaheim, washed

1 large bunch of fresh cilantros, rinsed and drained
5 large garlic cloves, peeled
1 teaspoon cumin
1 teaspoon salt
1/2 teaspoon black pepper
1/4 cup olive oil

Cut stems and remove seeds from the peppers, transfer to a food processor and add all other ingredients, mix for 3-4 minutes, open and scrape sides of the food processor, close and mix again. If the mixture is not smooth and thick add more olive oil 1 tablespoon at the time. Mix again to get a smooth consistency. Transfer to a container, cover with olive oil as an oxygen barrier. Store in the refrigerator, Schug is a hot spicy spread so use with cautious, this recipe yields one small 6oz. jar.

GARAM MASALA SPICE MIX — THE KING OF AROMA ⭐— SPECIALTY

1 teaspoon ground cinnamon or 1" long cinnamon stick
1/2 teaspoon ground cloves or 3 whole cloves
1/2 teaspoon black pepper or 3 black peppercorns
1/2 teaspoon ground cardamon or 2 black cardamon pods
2 teaspoons regular cumin, ground or 2 teaspoons black cumin seeds

If using the ready ground spices, mix well and transfer to a glass jar. If using the whole spices, grind in a spice grinder to get a powder consistency and transfer to a glass jar. Store in a dark cool place until use. This is a small amount spice mix, it is very dominant so use only 1-2 teaspoons or what the recipe calls for, store the remaining mixture for next use.

HARISSA SPREAD — MOROCCO, TUNISIA, ALGERIA, ISRAEL ⭐— SPECIALTY

1.1 pounds mixed ancho and California dry chilis
1.5 tablespoons ground cumin
1/2 cup extra virgin olive oil (cold press)
1/2 cup white vinegar
7-8 large fresh garlic cloves
1 teaspoon salt

Open dry chili peppers, get rid of the seeds and stems, soak in hot water for 1 hour, transfer to a colander to drain water. Place all ingredients in a food processor and grind for 3 minutes. Scrape sides of the food processor and use spatula to mix in pieces that need to be gridded more. Grind all content for another 5-7 minutes to get a smooth spread. Transfer to a glass container and drizzle top with extra olive oil to use as an oxygen barrier. This delicious spread will last as long as it is covered with olive oil, so keep adding olive oil after each use. Serve cold on sandwiches, use as a flavoring for every main dish, pasta, rice, and more. This recipe yields about 16-20 ounces jar.

LEKAMA — MAMA'S MEATBALLS SPICE MIX — MOROCCO ⭐— SPECIALTY

2 tablespoons ground Mace
1 tablespoon ground black pepper
1 teaspoon ground ginger
1 teaspoon ground cinnamon
1 tablespoon English pepper
1 tablespoon turmeric
1 whole nutmeg, ground

This spice mix was known as the main spice mix for meatball dishes, it is different than Ras Al Hanut which has a lot more spices and a large variety. Place all spices in a small jar and mix. Use as much as needed for different recipes to flavor meatball recipes.

MAGIC CHERMULA SAUCE FOR EVERY FISH DISH — MOROCCO, TUNISIA 🌺 —IN MEMORY

1/4 cup extra virgin olive oil
1 cup vinegar
1 tablespoon sweet or hot paprika
1 tablespoon cumin
4-5 large garlic cloves, minced
1/2 cup fresh cilantro, chopped
1 teaspoon salt
fish—any white fish such as sea bass, mahi mahi, tilapia, cod, trout

Get the Chermoula ready before you grill or fry the fish. Place all ingredients in a small bowl, mix well, let the sauce sit for at least an hour before serving. This sauce is great on grilled fish or fried. When the fish is ready, set it on a serving plate and drizzle the Chermoula on top of the fish. Let the marinade soak in the fish for at least 30 minutes before serving. Chermoula sauce allows you to serve the fish warm or cold. If you are serving the fish warm, drizzle the Chermoula on the fish and place in the oven for about 6 minutes right before serving. This recipe yields a Chermoula sauce for 1 medium fish.

OREGANO TAHINI — GREEK

1/2 cup sesame Tahini paste, raw (no roasted sesame paste)
2 tablespoons lemon juice
2-4 tablespoons water

1/4 teaspoon each salt and pepper
1 tablespoon fresh oregano leaves

In a small bowl mix Tahini paste and lemon juice, add 1 tablespoon water and start checking consistency. If Tahini is too thick add another 1 tablespoon water, mix again and check. If the consistency is to your likeness add the rest of the ingredients. Drizzle on the Greek Shawarma dish (see recipe) or serve as a dip. This recipe yields about 6-8 ounces Tahini sauce.

PILPELCHUMA PASTE TO FLAVOR MANY DISHES — TUNISIA, SYRIA, ALGERIA ⏰—QUICK & EASY

10 large garlic cloves peeled
5 tablespoons paprika (sweet or spicy)
1 tablespoon chili flax
1 tablespoon ground cumin
1/2 tablespoon caraway
1/2 cup extra virgin olive oil (cold press)

In a food processor add all ingredients and mix 3-4 minutes, scrape side of the mixer bowl and mix for another 3 minutes to get a smooth consistency. Transfer to a container, drizzle a little olive oil to create an oxygen barrier and refrigerate. Use 1 tablespoon for chicken, fish, or meat dishes. This recipe yields about 8 ounces spice mix, use only what the recipe calls for, usually 1 tablespoon in a dish or Tagine.

PUMPKIN BAKE SPICE MIX ⏰—QUICK & EASY

1 teaspoon ground cinnamon
1/4 teaspoon nutmeg
1/4 teaspoon ginger

1/4 teaspoon cloves

Place all ingredients in a small bowl, mix well to blend, use the amount that the recipe calls for. Store in an airtight glass container, in a dark cool place. This recipe yields about one amount for a pumpkin cake.

VILLAGE STYLE LABANE YOGURT CHEESE — ISRAEL, LEBANON, GREEK, CYPRUS ⏰—QUICK & EASY

2 pounds plain yogurt
1 teaspoon salt
1 large cheese cloth
colander
herbs to flavor—chives, basil, thyme, garlic
cold press olive oil to top labane

Place the plain yogurt in a large bowl, add salt and mix well. Place a colander on a large bowl and line it up with double layers of cheese cloth. Pour labane onto the cheese cloth, cover with a clear plastic wrap and refrigerate for 1 day. The next day remove clear plastic wrap and get rid of excess water in the bottom bowl. Tie the cheese cloth to make a kind of sack and return to colander, refrigerate for another day. Repeat like the first day, remove excess liquids from bottom bowl and return labane to the refrigerator. The labane might be ready after the 3rd day or the 4th day. When labane is ready, remove from cheese cloth by scraping it and transfer to a container. Drizzle extra virgin/cold press olive oil on labane to cover, the oil serves as an oxygen barrier. If you would like to flavor the labane, select chives, basil, thyme, garlic, and chop small, mix in the labane. Refrigerate and serve cold. This recipe yields about 30-35 ounces of labane cheese spread.

YAFFA'S AWARD-WINNING LEMON SPREAD 🏅—AWARD WINNING

3 lemons with very thick peel, no seeds
2 garlic cloves
1 teaspoon salt
1/2 cup olive oil, cold press

This dish is great with steamed vegetables, especially the ones you don't like. Place lemons in a large bowl with cold water, brush lemon skin with vegetable brush. Leave skin on, use a sharp knife to thinly slice lemons and get rid of all seeds. Place each slice against the light to better check if you missed any seeds. Place all ingredients including seedless lemons in a food processor, grind on high speed. Scrape sides of mixing bowl to help all ingredients blend in. Mix again on high speed for 3-5 minutes, spread should be smooth. Taste to see if needs more salt, mix again for 2-3 minutes. Transfer to a container, drizzle olive oil on top to serve as an oxygen barrier. Refrigerate, serve cold. This recipe yields about 12-15 ounces of lemon spread.

YAFFA'S BEST EVER TAHINI

2 cups ice water or cold club soda water
1 1/2 cups raw Tahini (not roasted)
1/2 cup freshly squeezed lemon juice
1 fresh garlic clove, peeled
1 teaspoon salt
fresh parsley, leaves only for decoration

In a food processor place ice water first, then add raw Tahini, salt, lemon juice, and garlic, mix on high speed for 2 minutes, open and check consistency and flavor. If Tahini is liquid enough do not add water. If Tahini seems to be very thick and creamy add 1 tablespoon ice water and mix again. Tahini tends to thicken a little the next day. Mix for another 2-3 minutes and transfer to a container. Before serving decorate with a little parsley, leaves only. This recipe yields about 25-30 ounces tahini sauce.

YAFFA'S DELIGHTFUL CELERIAC ROOT LEMON DIP 🧡—HEART HEALTHY

1 cup of chef Yaffa's lemon spread and dip (see recipe in This and That category)
1 medium celery root
1/4 cup freshly squeezed lemon juice
1/4 cup olive oil
1/2 teaspoon each salt and white pepper

Use vegetable brush to brush off dust and dirt from celeriac root, use a potato peeler to peel off the outer layer of celeriac root, if need brush those stubborn cracks that have more dirt in them. Chop the celeriac root to small pieces, transfer all ingredients to a food processor and mix on medium speed for 2-3 minutes. Scrape the walls of the mixing bowl and grind again on high speed for another 4-5 minutes. The spread will be somewhat grainy but naturally, transfer to a container and refrigerate. Serve cold with dipping vegetables such as carrots, celery, and bell pepper, this recipe yields about 2-26 ounces celeriac dip; it depends on the size of the celery root.

YAFFA'S FORMULA FOR — NEVER STICK BAKED FOOD ⭐— SPECIALTY

1/2 cup Crisco shortening
1/2 cup flour
1/2 cup vegetable oil

Place all ingredients in a small glass container, mix well, preferably with a whisk, cover. This formula is best when made on the day of the baking but can be stored for a second use if refrigerated. It can be stored for 3-4 days. This recipe yields for about 4-5 baking pans.

YAFFA'S HOMEMADE ZAA'TAR MIX ⭐—SPECIALTY

1 tablespoon dry thyme or dry oregano or dry marjoram
1 tablespoon sumac powder
1 tablespoon sesame seeds

If choosing the thyme za'atar combination, use it for cooking dishes, if choosing the oregano or marjoram combination, use it for both hot and cold dishes. Combine equal amounts of these ingredients and transfer to a glass jar. Store in dark cool dishes. Za'atar is considered a medicinal in the Mediterranean and Balkan countries. Use this mixture to flavor your salads and side dishes, it is a dominant flavor so sprinkle it lightly on a dish, about 1 teaspoon per recipe, this mixture yields 4-5 teaspoons.

YAFFA'S MAIN DISH MEAT MARINADE ⭐—SPECIALTY

2 teaspoons cumin
1 1/2 teaspoons coriander
1/4 teaspoon cayenne pepper, or more if desired
2 1/2 teaspoons sweet paprika
1/2 teaspoon ground pepper
7 tablespoons extra virgin olive oil
1/4 cup fresh lemon juice
2-3 tablespoons garlic, minced
5 tablespoons fresh cilantro, chopped

Place all ingredients in a small container, mix well, allow ingredients to sit for 30 minutes for the flavors to blend. This marinade is great for all kinds of meat and poultry, and fish as well. This marinade is especially delicious for grilling, this recipe yields about 16 ounces marinade which is usually good for two uses.

YAFFA'S REFRESHING AVOCADO SALAD DRESSING ⏰—QUICK & EASY

2/3 cup olive oil
2 tablespoons white vinegar
2 tablespoons apple cider vinegar
1 1/2 teaspoons Dijon mustard
1 teaspoon salt

1/4 teaspoon black pepper

Mix all dressing ingredients well, add avocado cubes, lettuce, and cherry tomatoes, store in a refrigerator, serve cold. This recipe yields about 16 ounces of dressing.

YAFFA'S SAVORY WHEATFOR SHABBAT CHAMIN, SCHINA, DEFINA, CHULENT FOREVER SHABBAT DISH 🌺—IN MEMORY

1 pound whole wheat (or brown rice if you are gluten free)
1 tablespoon sweet paprika
1 teaspoon cumin
3 tablespoons vegetable oil
4 garlic cloves, minced
1 teaspoon salt
3 tablespoons homemade Harissa (see recipe in This and That category)
remaining garlic pieces from the 2 whole heads (The small pieces of garlic cloves that you sliced from the garlic heads that go in the chamin/cholent recipe, see recipe in the main dishes category.)
1 dry chili pepper (ancho or California)—low spicy
1 cup water
1 cookie bag

In a saucepan place garlic and oil, cook for a minute. Add harissa and spices simmer for 1-2 minutes, add whole wheat and cook for 5 minutes while stirring constantly. Add water and bring to a boil, reduce and cover, cook for 20 minutes on simmer. Transfer wheat and liquids to the cookie bag, fold like a log to secure from leaking, use a fork to poke several holes on the top part of the log, set aside until the rest of the chamin pot is ready to be cooked. This recipe yields one wheat bag that goes in the chamin/cholent pot.

YAFFA'S SHAWARMA SPICE MIX ⭐—SPECIALTY

1/4-1/2 teaspoon each salt and pepper
1 tablespoon garam masala mix (see recipe in This and That category)
1 tablespoon chicken consume or beef flavoring
1 1/2 tablespoons curry powder

Mix all dry ingredients, store in a glass jar in a dark cool place. This Shawarma spice mix will work great on lamb, chicken, or the traditional turkey Shawarma. This recipe yields amount enough for 1-2 recipes.

YAFFA'S TZAZIKI YOGURT SAUCE — GREEK ⭐—SPECIALTY

1 1/4 cups yogurt
2 fresh garlic cloves, minced
2 tablespoons extra virgin olive oil
2 tablespoons fresh dill, chopped
1/4 teaspoon black pepper
1/2 teaspoon salt
1 cucumber, small, skin peeled

Shred cucumber, squeeze all liquid, combine all ingredients in a mixing bowl, refrigerate for 1 hour before serving. Serve chilled, this recipe yields about 20-25oz. jar of delicious Tzatziki sauce.

USEFUL NOTES

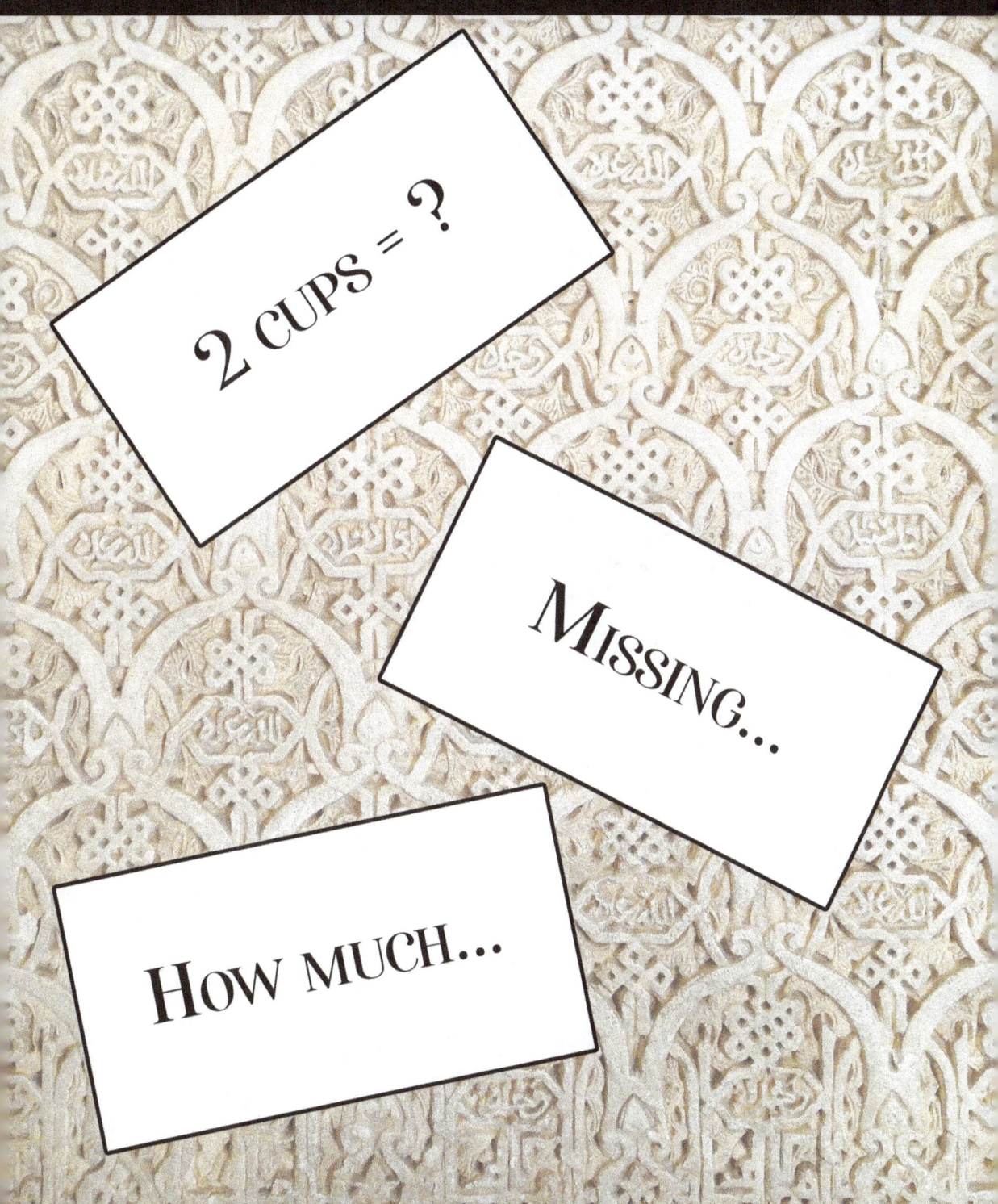

CONVERSIONS

MEASUREMENTS

a pinch.............................1/8 teaspoon or less
3 teaspoons ....1 tablespoon
4 tablespoons ....1/4 cup
8 tablespoons ....1/2 cup
12 tablespoons.......................................3/4 cup
16 tablespoons.......................................1 cup
2 cups...1 pint
4 cups ....1 quart
4 quarts...1 gallon
8 quarts...1 peck
4 pecks ....1 bushel are estimates
16 ounces...1 pound
32 ounces ....1 quart
1 ounce liquid ....2 tablespoons
8 ounces liquid ....1 cup
Use standard measuring spoons and cups. All measurements are level.

C° TO F° CONVERSION

120° C.............................250° F
140° C.............................275° F
150° C.............................300° F
160° C.............................325° F
180° C.............................350° F
190° C.............................375° F
200° C.............................400° F
220° C.............................425° F
230° C.............................450° F

SUBSTITUTIONS

INGREDIENT...QUANTITY...SUBSTITUTE

baking powder ...1 teaspoon ...1/4 teaspoon baking soda plus 1/2 teaspoon cream of tartar

chocolate ...1 square (1 oz.) ... 3 or 4 tablespoon cocoa plus 1 tablespoon butter

cornstarch ...1 tablespoon ....2 tablespoon flour or 2 teaspoon quick-cooking tapioca

cracker crumbs ...3/4 cup ....1 c. breadcrumbs

dates ...1 pound ....1 1/2 c. dates, pitted and cut

dry mustard ....1 teaspoon ....1 tablespoon prepared mustard

flour, self-rising...1 cup .....1 cup all-purpose flour, 1/2 teaspoon salt, and 1 teaspoon baking powder

herbs, fresh ...1 tablespoon ...1 teaspoon dried herb

ketchup or chili sauce ...1 cup ....1 cup tomato sauce plus 1/2 cup sugar and 2 tablespoons vinegar (for use in cooking)

milk, sour ...1 cup ...1 tablespoon lemon juice or vinegar plus sweet milk to make 1 cup (let stand 5 minutes) milk, whole ...1 cup......1/2 cup evaporated milk plus 1/2 cup water

min. marshmallows ...10 ...1 large marshmallow

onion, fresh .....1 small.....1 tablespoon instant minced onion, rehydrated

sugar, brown ...1/2 cup ... 2 tablespoons molasses and 1/2 cup granulated sugar

sugar, powdered...1 cup...1 cup granulated sugar plus 1 teaspoon cornstarch

tomato juice ...1 cup...1/2 cup tomato sauce plus 1/2 cup water

When substituting cocoa for chocolate in cakes, the amount of flour must be reduced. Brown and white sugars usually can be interchanged.

FOOD QUANTITY YIELD

apple.....1 medium.....1 cup

banana, mashed.....1 medium.....1/3 cup

bread.....1 1/2 slices.....1 cup soft crumb

bread.....1 slice.....1/4 cup fine, dry crumbs

butter.....1 stick or 1/4.....1/2 cup

cheese, American, cubed.....1 pound.....2 2/3 cups

American, grated.....1 pound.....5 cups

cream cheese.....3-ounce package.....6 2/3 tablespoons

chocolate, bitter.....1 square.....1 ounce

cocoa.....1 pound.....4 cups

coconut.....1 1/2 pounds package.....2 2/3 cups

coffee, ground.....1 pound.....5 cups

cornmeal.....1 pound.....3 cups

cornstarch.....1 pound.....3 cups

crackers, graham.....14 squares.....1 cup fine crumb

saltine.....28 crackers.....1 cup fine crumbs

egg.....4-5 whole.....1 cup

whites.....8-10.....1 cup

yolks.....10-12.....1 cup

evaporated milk.....1 cup.....3 cups whipped

flour, cake, sifted.....1 pound.....4 1/2 cups

rye.....1 pound.....5 cups

white, sifted.....1 pound.....4 cups

white, unsifted.....1 pound.....3 3/4 cups

gelatin, flavored.....3 1/4 ounces.....1/2 cup

gelatin, unflavored.....1/4 ounce.....1 tablespoon

lemon.....1 medium.....3 tablespoons juice

marshmallows.....16.....1/4 pound

noodles, cooked.....8-ounce package.....7 cups

noodles, uncooked.....4 ounces (1 1/2 cups).....2-3 cups cooked

macaroni, cooked.....8-ounce package.....6 cups

macaroni, uncooked.....4 ounces (1 1/4 cups).....2 1/4 cups cooked

spaghetti, uncooked.....7 ounces.....4 cups cooked

nuts, chopped.....1/4 pound.....1 cup

almonds.....1 pound.....3 1/2 cups

walnuts, broken.....1 pound.....3 cups

walnuts, unshelled.....1 pound.....1 1/2 to 1 3/4 cups

onion.....1 medium.....1/2 cup

orange.....3-4 medium.....1 cup juice

raisins.....1 pound.....3 1/2 cups

rice, brown.....1 cup.....4 cups cooked

rice, converted.....1 cup.....3 1/2 cups cooked

rice, regular.....1 cup.....3 cups cooked

rice, wild.....1 cup.....4 cups cooked

sugar, brown.....1 pound.....2 1/2 cups

sugar, powdered.....1 pound.....3 1/2 cups

sugar, white.....1 pound.....2 cups

vanilla wafers.....22.....1 cup fine crumbs

zwieback, crumbled.....4.....1 cup

ABOUT THE AUTHOR

Nice to meet you, I'm Chef Yaffa!

I was born in Israel & grew up in a large Moroccan Jewish family of 10 siblings. When I was 5 we lost my father to a heart disease and I watched my Mom struggling , working very hard to raise us. My Mom used to stay up late to make sure that lunch was ready for the next day while she was at work, so I used to stay with her & help her cook so that she can finally go to bed to rest. As a teenager I was already cooking and baking at home to take off the load from my Mom.

As a young Mom myself I worked as a personal chef for many years & later on opened my own restaurant & a wedding/Bar Mitzvah catering named- Yaffa's Savory, & loved the community that we created. Sephardic Jewish community in America is less known like the Ashkenazi Jewish community, so I felt the need to introduce this side of the Jewish community to my fans & help them learn the history of a dish, holidays in the Sephardic community and serve as a bridge between the two communities.

On my Youtube channel viewers can explore foods from all the jewish communities that are considered Sephardic & Mizrachi around the Mediterranean sea. Today I offer culinary workshops on Zoom worldwide & in private, and upload a video a week to my youtube channel.

As my channel grew I started with your help to support three charities (St. Jude Children's Research Hospital, Wounded Warrior Project and International Fellowship of Christians and Jews) that are very close to my heart.

My true enjoyment is baking cookies with my three granddaughters, Lyla, Noa, and baby Orli.

https://www.sephardicflavors.com/

f facebook.com/yaffa.hanouna.1

◉ instagram.com/sephardic_flavors

▶ youtube.com/@sephardicflavors